DISCOVERING THE JOY THAT DEFINED THE FIRST BELIEVERS

JARED MITZELFELT

LUCIDBOOKS

Marked by Joy: Discovering the Joy that Defined the First Believers
Copyright © 2025 by Jared Mitzelfelt
Published by Lucid Books in Houston, TX
www.LucidBooks.com

All rights reserved. No part of this publication may be reproduced, stored in a retrieval system, or transmitted in any form by any means, electronic, mechanical, photocopy, recording, or otherwise, without the prior permission of the publisher, except as provided for by USA copyright law.

Unless otherwise indicated, scripture quotations are taken from the ESV® Bible (The Holy Bible, English Standard Version®), copyright © 2001 by Crossway, a publishing ministry of Good News Publishers. Used by permission. All rights reserved.

Scripture quotations marked (CSB) are from the Holman Christian Standard Bible®, Copyright © 2017 by Holman Bible Publishers. Used by permission.

Scripture quotations marked (MSG) are taken from THE MESSAGE, copyright © 1993, 2002, 2018 by Eugene H. Peterson. Used by permission of NavPress. All rights reserved. Represented by Tyndale House Publishers, Inc.

Scripture quotations marked (NIV) are taken from the Holy Bible, New International Version®, NIV®. Copyright ©1973, 1978, 1984, 2011 by Biblica, Inc.™ Used by permission of Zondervan. All rights reserved worldwide. www.zondervan.com The "NIV" and "New International Version" are trademarks registered in the United States Patent and Trademark Office by Biblica, Inc.™

ISBN: 978-1-63296-766-4
eISBN: 978-1-63296-767-1

Special Sales: Most Lucid Books titles are available in special quantity discounts. Custom imprinting or excerpting can also be done to fit special needs. Contact Lucid Books at Info@LucidBooks.com

To Samantha, Ellie, and Ethan,
You make my joy complete. I love you so much.

Table of Contents

Chapter One: Pursuing Joy Begins — 1

Chapter Two: Joy in the Bible — 19

Chapter Three: Joy in Psychology — 41

Chapter Four: Defining Joy — 59

Chapter Five: Joy Idols — 79

Chapter Six: Abiding Joy — 103

Chapter Seven: Joy Thieves — 131

Chapter Eight: Complete Joy — 155

Chapter Nine: Joy in Suffering — 179

Chapter Ten: Joy is Contagious — 203

Endnotes — 227

CHAPTER ONE
Pursuing Joy Begins

My family gets sick all the time. Honestly, it's become a family activity. Instead of tossing a ball around, we toss around viruses. You may share memes in your family group chat; we share Mucinex and Tylenol. We have a beautiful four-year-old daughter named Ellie, who is a courier of all sorts of germs. Between church and her preschool, she regularly brings something home with her. My wife Samantha and I also both work on staff at a church in Round Rock, Texas, where she directs our kid's ministry, and I pastor our young adult ministry. Between the three of us and all the exposure, we are doomed to catch something regularly. And once one of us catches something, it's only a matter of time until it strikes all of us like the angel of death. Too strong? It feels like that sometimes.

There were a few months in the fall when I had bronchitis. My coughing was so aggressive that I severely injured my ribs on the right side of my body. I didn't know what to think, whether it was a pulled muscle, cracked cartilage, or broken ribs. All I knew was it hurt bad! I went to my doctor, and she ordered X-rays. She said, "Because you're a young adult male and not an eighty-year-old woman, I don't think you broke any ribs. But I want to rule that out officially." So, I got the X-rays done, and the next day, I got a call from the doctor with shocking news. I broke three ribs! After getting that news, I reflected on my doctor's previous comment. Does this mean I have the body of an eighty-year-old woman, or do I have super-human strength to break my own ribs? I choose the latter. I asked my doctor what I needed to do to heal. She said, "Stop coughing." Got it, doc. I'll stop that immediately.

So, after months of recovering from breaking my ribs, here we were, sick again. Ellie got sick on Sunday; Sam came down on Monday, and yours truly on Tuesday. Cue the angel of death. Fever, chills, aches, sore throat, headache; you name it, we had it. To make things more complicated, we had our two-month-old son, Ethan, who we were trying to protect from getting sick. The flu and infants don't mix well. We had to strategically decide how to prevent Ethan from exposure while we all tried to heal. If Covid taught us anything, it taught us how to quarantine! We decided to isolate me in our upstairs office until my symptoms subsided. I spent the next 24 hours in that room feeling bad and frustrated. *Why does this always happen to us? Why can't we go one month without getting sick?* That night, I laid on my deflated air mattress with a deflated spirit.

The next morning, my fever broke (not my ribs this time), and I felt a little better. Since I was already in the office, I decided to go ahead and get some work done. I was scheduled to preach the next day at our young adult gathering that meets on Thursday nights. As a ministry, we were teaching through the letter of 1 Peter.

The Apostle Peter wrote this letter to Christians in Asia Minor, now modern-day Turkey. These Christians were feeling pressure from Roman society for their faith and were suffering because of it. Romans persecuted Christians because they wouldn't participate in Roman holidays, worship Roman gods, or profess Caesar as Lord. The Romans pressured the Christians to conform to the cultural norm, or else they would make their lives miserable. They would deny Christians business, which affected their ability to buy and sell to make money. If you don't make money, you can't have a house, pay taxes, and buy food. This is not to mention the constant public shaming, false charges, and, in the worst cases, imprisonment and death.[1] To sum it up, the believers in this region were going through it.

So, Peter writes this letter to these suffering believers to encourage them. He knew what it was like to deny Jesus, and from experience, he wanted to tell them it is worse to deny Jesus than to suffer because of Him. With that in mind, I focused my attention on studying 1 Peter 1:3-12 to prepare to preach. After several hours of reading and studying, verses 6-9 particularly grabbed my attention. We read:

"In all this you greatly rejoice, though now for a little while you may have had to suffer grief in all kinds of trials. These have come so that the proven genuineness of your faith—of greater worth than gold, which perishes even though refined by fire—may result in praise, glory and honor when Jesus Christ is revealed. Though you have not seen him, you love him; and even though you do not see him now, you believe in him and are filled with an inexpressible and glorious joy, for you are receiving the end result of your faith, the salvation of your souls."

I have read this passage numerous times before but never noticed I was reading it incorrectly. I have always read verse six as a command. It is as if Peter were saying, "Since you are going through trials, you should rejoice in all this." But that's not what Peter is saying. Verse six is not a command but an indicative statement, which means he's describing them. He's not telling them what they should do. Rather, he's describing what they are already doing. He's describing these Christians as being joyful in the midst of their trials. What's interesting is that Peter has likely never met these people before. So, how did he know they were joyful? Because joy is what marked the first-century Christians.

MARKED BY JOY

In the apostle's day, if you were a follower of Jesus, it was assumed that you were filled with joy. Peter expounded on that in verses 8 and 9, "Though you have not seen him, you love him; and even though you do not see him now, you believe in him and are filled with an *inexpressible and glorious joy.*" As I meditated on this passage, I felt myself sinking into my desk chair with a heavy heart. Joy marked the first-century Christian, but does it mark the twenty-first-century Christian? As I considered that, I started to reflect on my own life. Does joy mark me? Am I filled with an inexpressible and glorious joy that Peter is describing?

With sadness, my answer was no. To be transparent, what often describes me is anxiety, anger, and a negative attitude. I overthink things all the time and always assume the worst. When I'm stressed, I lash out at the ones I love. I'm easily annoyed when I'm inconvenienced or when something doesn't go my way. My sins and shortcomings are ever present in my mind, which leads to a constant feeling of shame. I believe I've experienced joyful moments, but I wouldn't say it marked my life. Joy wasn't as consistent as it seemed it should be as a believer. Something was deeply wrong. God revealed to me in that office that my body wasn't just sick, but so was my heart.

How about you? Does joy mark you?

I encourage you to take some time to reflect on this. You may confidently answer yes or no. But if you're unsure, ask a few people who know you well. It would be helpful to give them permission to be completely honest. Naturally, people are not going to say negative things about you even though it may be the truth. After this, you will have your answer. If you're like me and your answer is no, don't be discouraged. The truth is you're not alone.

WHAT MARKS US TODAY

Gallup released in 2023 that the world has been experiencing record-breaking sadness, stress, anxiety, and depression compared to the previous 17 years.[2] Recently, Oracle conducted a research study called "The Happiness Report" that found 45% of people have not felt true happiness for more than two years, and 25% were unsure if they have ever felt true happiness[3] (Note: Most studies do not use "joy"). According to the CDC, as of October

2023, 30% of adults in the US reported symptoms of anxiety and depression. The highest rate was found in adults ages 18-29, which came in at 45%.[4] That means almost half of young adults in the US today are struggling with their mental health.

Mental health professionals were optimistic that people would bounce back from the pandemic, but that has not been the case. The increase in mental health issues has led to an increase in substance abuse and suicide. The National Center for Drug Abuse Statistics states that 50% of people over the age of 12 have used illicit drugs.[5] Suicide rates increased 37% between 2000-2018, peaked in 2021, and have steadily increased year after year since.[6] Overall, nearly half of the US population would agree with these statements: "I often feel lonely," "I have no sense of purpose," and "I do not enjoy my life."

You may think, "Well, those stats are surveying the nation and the world. What about Christians?" Recently, a UK study surveyed Christians and church leaders from various denominations. They found that 43% of Christians have struggled with their mental health issues in the last few years.[7] The next time you sit in a Sunday church service, look at your row. Four out of ten people in your row think negatively about themselves, their lives, and the world around them. You may understand because you are one of them. The overall statistics show that Christians are not exempt from the mental health crisis but rather are very much a part of it.

Now, this does not mean the other six out of ten are not struggling. What I have observed is that the majority of believers are worn out physically, spiritually, and emotionally from life. Think about what we say when we interact with one another.

"Hey, how's it going?" The common response used to be, "Good, I'm just busy." But recently, the response has changed. Now it's "Good, just I'm *tired*." I don't think that change is random; I believe it is a result.

Because of our busyness, we are worn out. Our lifestyles demand more than what our mind, body, and soul can give. We are an overworked, overcommitted, and over-entertained people who are just trying to keep up with the pace of culture. Instead of making changes, we continue to be busy and tired. We are just trying to get to the next thing on our busy calendars without falling apart. Because we are so tired, we are easily irritated, frustrated, and angered. This lifestyle is detrimental to our well-being, and it produces little to no joy. In his book *The Ruthless Elimination of Hurry*, John Mark Comer wrote, "Love, *joy*, and peace are at the heart of all Jesus is trying to grow in the soil of your life. And all three are incompatible with hurry."[8] In other words, a hurried life doesn't produce joy; rather, it prevents us from it.

Many of us are worn out from hurrying, but others are worn out from hurting. These are the things that weren't on our busy calendars. It's the cancer diagnosis you didn't see coming. It's the physical pain you walk around with every day. It's the grief you have because of your loved one who died, and you miss so much. It's the auto-immune disorder diagnosis that has dramatically altered your lifestyle. It's the miscarriage you thought would never happen to you. It's the sadness you feel watching a loved one suffer without any signs of getting better. It's the heartbreak you feel because your marriage is falling apart, and you're not sure you're going to make it. It's the devastating news that you or your spouse lost a job, and you're not sure what you're going to do next. It's the internal pain you feel from your past trauma, and you're not sure you'll ever overcome it. It's the loneliness you feel because you have no real friends, and it seems like no one sees you or cares about you. Life is hard, and life hurts. I think of Eugene Peterson's rendering of Lamentations 3:28: "Life is heavy and hard to take" (The Message). In these seasons, finding any joy in life is difficult. The past haunts, the present hurts, and the future seems hopeless. We are weary from the weight of our sadness and suffering.

Something else I've observed from hurried and hurting people is a rise of pessimism in the church. This is more than just being a glass-half-empty person or a Debbie downer (I'm so sorry to all the Debbie's out there!). This pessimism comes across as being overly critical and outwardly cynical. We're critical of unbelievers who are different from us. Whether generational, political, religious, or lifestyle differences, we view others as enemies to fight against instead of neighbors to fight for. But this criticalness isn't just in the world; it's in the church. There is so much division today about the style of worship and theological convictions. Denominations have become church silos where we choose not to interact with one another. But when we do, it ends up being a debate stage where we disagree and disrespect one another. Does that sound like joy to you?

This critical and cynical heart is evident not only in the church at large but also in our local churches. We will complain about worship. It's too loud. We didn't like the song selections. We like hymns instead of contemporary or contemporary instead of hymns. We'll talk at lunch about our opinions of the sermon. But that's not the only thing talked about at lunch, is it? We gossip about who was at church and why others weren't at church. We talk about what people wore and what others said in our small groups. Even the people who came up for prayer during the service become a topic of conversation. More often than not, these conversations are negative. Even when God is working, many of us default to being cynical. This is a problem today. After reflection and research, I've concluded that I'm not the only one who is sick, but the church is sick, too.

WHAT HAPPENED TO JOY?

When we come to church on Sunday morning, we sing worship songs about the joy we have. We listen to sermons about the joy we should have. In our Bible studies, we read about the joy others had. And though we sing, listen, and read about joy, the vast majority in the room don't actually have it. What is supposed to mark us as a people is sadly absent. There is an incredible disconnect between what we are saying and reading and what we are experiencing. Because of this, the Yale Center of Faith and Culture, a part of the Yale Divinity School, conducted a project called "The Theology of Joy and Good Life" to explore this issue. They summarized the state of joy this way:

> Joy is fundamental to human existence and well-being, yet it is an elusive phenomenon that resists definition. For more than two millennia, the articulation and cultivation of joy was at the center of Jewish and Christian scripture, theology, and practices— [But] the very idea of joy has all but disappeared from modern theological reflection, is all but ignored by the social sciences, and is

increasingly absent from lived experience. The consequence is a "flattening out," a "graying," of human life and communities—abundance of entertainment notwithstanding—and a sharp bloom of individual and communal dysfunction.⁹

This summary is spot on. Joy is something we all desire but struggle to obtain. So, what is the solution? The first step is determining what joy is, but that's not as easy as it sounds.

DEFINING JOY IS DIFFICULT

As the Theology of Joy states, joy is an elusive phenomenon that resists definition. That's a fancy way of saying joy is difficult to define. Is it an emotion? Is it a positive attitude? Is it a personality trait? Is it a state of being? Is it happiness? Do we have the capability to choose joy, or is it something out of our control? The point is it's challenging to have something when you don't know what it is. For the next few moments, think of how you define joy and write it down in the space below.

_____

_____

If you asked ten people to define joy, you would get ten different answers. Out of curiosity, I did this! I asked ten believers of different ages, from eighteen to eighty. Here are their definitions:

1. Joy is permanent happiness.
2. Joy is genuine satisfaction only found in Jesus.
3. Joy is finding fulfillment or contentment in my current situation.

4. Joy comes from God and isn't dependent on circumstances.
5. Joy gives us a disposition and judgment that all our decisions will bring glory to God irrespective of what will happen to us (can you tell this was a quantum physicist?)
6. Joy is a fruit of good spiritual living.
7. Joy is peaceful happiness.
8. Joy is a deep inner feeling from God.
9. Joy is a godly, positive attitude.
10. Joy is an emotion that is experienced, not by choice.

How similar was your definition to these? This exercise was fun but also insightful.

Why did all ten people have different definitions of joy? It's because our definition of joy is an interpretation of three major influences.

Interpreting Personal Experience
First, we define joy by interpreting our personal experiences. When I asked Rene to define joy, she answered, "peaceful happiness." I asked her why she described joy that way. She told me about the time she traveled through the desert of West Texas. She reflected on the vast, rugged landscape, the dryness of the air, and the warm hues of the sunsets. While driving, there would be times when the only living souls in sight were her and her husband and a coyote in the distance. When she thinks about joy, she thinks of that place, and the way she felt in that place was peaceful happiness.

This is what many of us do when we try to define joy. We reflect on time(s) when we've experienced what we believe is joy and try to put into words what it felt like. Your place might not be the desert (I'm more of an ocean guy myself), but maybe it's eating your favorite food, going out with friends, or spending daily time in the Word. For Rene, joy feels like peaceful happiness, but to others, joy may feel like contentment, a sense of belonging, deep satisfaction, or fulfillment. Sometimes, it's even difficult to put into words how we feel. That's why Karen described joy as "a deep inner feeling from God." We know something is there, but it's hard to put into words what it is. But are these feelings joy? That's something we must consider.

Interpreting Scripture

Second, we define joy by interpreting Scripture. This is good! As Bible-believing Christians, Scripture should be our guide in defining joy. However, even the Scriptures will lead believers to different conclusions about what joy is. Because we interpret the Scriptures differently, we also interpret joy differently.

First, some interpret joy as an *emotion*. You can't read the Psalms without feeling the emotions of the writers. It's as if we are reading their journals reflecting on God's goodness in their life, and they are overflowing with joy (Ps. 32:11, Ps. 45:1, Ps. 71:23). They can't help themselves but to sing, praise, and worship. They even invite others to join them in their joy (Ps. 33:1, Ps.100:1)! That's why my friend Nate defined joy as "an emotion that is experienced, not by choice." In other words, joy is our natural emotional response to God and can't be manipulated or forced. John Piper holds this view of joy, as he says, "Joy is not an act of will-power, but a spontaneous, emotional response of the heart."[10]

Second, some interpret joy as an *attitude*. The basis for this view is in passages that command believers to have joy

(1 Thess. 5:16, Phil. 4:4, Rom. 12:12). We can't command or force emotional responses; they just naturally happen. For example, I can't command you to be angry. Instead, something has to happen to make you angry, like being cut off in traffic. Just me? This logic then applies to these commands about joy in Scripture. Naturally, you can't force yourself to be joyful. Therefore, believers rule out joy as an emotion but conclude it must be an attitude. In fact, a popular belief is that you can choose joy regardless of how you feel or your circumstances. Even if you get cut off in traffic, you can choose joy! Kay Warren, co-founder of Saddleback Church and author of the book *Choose Joy*, says, "If we are going to experience joy in this lifetime, there's only one possible way: We will have to choose it."[11] In other words, joy is an act of our willpower, and it's our responsibility to choose it daily, no matter the circumstances.

Third, some interpret joy as an *attribute*. This interpretation ties back to Peter's description of the believers in Asia Minor at the beginning of this chapter. Joy is what marked these people. It's what made them distinct. Joy seems to be a state of being that comes from the presence of the Holy Spirit in our life (Galatians 5:22). Joy isn't something we do; it's who we become. John Mark Comer, who holds this view, says, "All three [love, joy, and peace] are more than just emotions; they are overall conditions of the heart…they are the kinds of people we become through our apprenticeship to Jesus, who embodies all three ad infinitum."[12] As we follow Christ, the Holy Spirit transforms us into a joyful person like our Lord. Therefore, joy is not just an emotion we experience or an attitude we choose but an attribute of who we are.

So, how do we reconcile these verses and views that seem to contradict one another? Keep in mind these are interpretations. We are trying to make sense of something complex with the evidence we have. Our temptation is to "pick a side" that makes the most sense to us, but then we don't consider the Scriptural evidence for the other views. Like any investigation, I believe each piece of evidence points us closer to the truth about joy.

Adopting Other's Interpretation

Third, we define joy by adopting someone else's interpretation. Our views are easily influenced by others, whether we are aware of it or not. We often adopt our views from parents, friends, family, church members, and pastors. Today, we even have our favorite well-known preachers and teachers whom we follow via social media, books, and YouTube. Because we like them, we naturally adopt their interpretations. None of these influences are inherently bad, but the danger is that we adopt their interpretations without investigating for ourselves.

A classic example in the church today is the distinction between happiness and joy. Almost every time I ask someone to define joy, the first thing they say is, "Well, it's not happiness." Then they'll say something like, "Happiness is circumstantial, and joy is not," or "Happiness is temporary, and joy is permanent," or "Happiness is worldly, joy is godly." You can see renditions of these in a couple of our definitions above.

What's interesting is the Bible actually doesn't make a distinction between joy and happiness. Also, before the twentieth century, there is no evidence of scholars, preachers, or teachers who made this distinction either.[13] That means this idea has only existed for about a hundred years. This distinction was made sometime in the twentieth century, and others have adopted it, even today. The question is, is it the truth? At this point, I'm not going to give my thoughts on this just yet (stay tuned), but this has influenced many believers' views of joy.

CONCLUSION

Are you confused? Are you not sure what to believe? That's exactly the point. The church as a whole is very confused. Think about it this way: because we have different definitions of joy when you hear a sermon about joy, you are likely interpreting the message differently than the person sitting next to you. In fact, your whole row is interpreting it differently! And many of these views contradict one another. Some believe joy is an emotion; others do not. Some believe you can choose joy; others do not. Some believe joy is a type of happiness; others do not. The point is that joy is one of the most misunderstood aspects of the Christian faith in the church today. If we don't know what it truly is, then we won't know where to find it and how to have it.

One time, I was getting ready to give Ethan a bottle and needed a boppy. For those who don't know, a boppy is a "C" shaped pillow that's helpful for feeding babies. Ellie takes a lot of pride in being a big helper. She is our runner for when we need diapers, bibs, or wipes. So, as I was getting ready to feed Ethan his bottle, I asked Ellie, "Can you go upstairs and get the boppy." She responds with excitement, "Yes! I'll be right back!" She ran upstairs as fast as her little legs could. Moments later, she returned downstairs with a burp cloth. I say, "Ellie, I need the boppy, not a burp cloth. Go get me the boppy, please." She said,

"Okay, sorry, I'll be right back!" So, she runs upstairs again. Moments later, she returned downstairs again, but this time she had a pacifier! I say, slightly frustrated, "Ellie, are you listening to me? I need the boppy!" Then Ellie replies, "Sorry, Daddy, I don't know what a boppy is!"

At that moment, I assumed Ellie knew what a boppy was, but she didn't. She was going upstairs to familiar places and guessing what the boppy was. She was so excited to be helpful, but she didn't take the time to ask me what a boppy was and where to find it. So, after laughing together and sharing a hug, I told her what the boppy looked like and where to find it. Then, she was successful!

This story is a picture of what has happened in the church. At large, the church has assumed that all believers know what joy is, but the truth is we don't. So, when we are told that we should have joy, we go to familiar places. We reflect on personal experiences, reference Scripture, and recount what we've read and heard from others. From here, we apply what we know. We try to recreate feelings from the past, have a positive attitude, do things that make us happy, or increase our spiritual disciplines. After pursuing joy, we realize that what we found wasn't it. Then we're left confused. *Why don't I have joy? Is something wrong with me? How am I supposed to have joy in my suffering?* I understand. I've been there.

Like Ellie, we have been running and trying to figure things out on our own, and it's left us lost and empty. The better option is to slow down and ask the Lord for help. I believe Jesus desires to restore joy in His church, and He is ready and willing to reveal to us what joy is, where to find it, and how to have it in our lives. But it's not just going to happen. We have to pursue joy with Him.

I wrote this book to bring clarity to the confusion about joy. I went into this project not having all the answers but instead lots of questions. The desire to know the truth about joy drove me to explore the Scriptures, meet with social science professionals, and listen to faithful saints. I'm confident this book will provide clarity and practicality to help you have the joy-filled life you desire. My prayer is when you finish this book, joy will mark you. Are you ready to start your pursuit of joy? Let's begin!

REFLECTION AND DISCUSSION QUESTIONS

1. Does joy mark your life? What would you say marks you?
2. What are the top three things that describe you?
3. What is causing you to hurry and hurt today? How do you feel?
4. How do you define joy?
5. Of the three influencers (personal experience, Scripture, others' interpretation), what has had the most influence on your view of joy?
6. Can you recall a time when you think you've experienced joy?

CHAPTER TWO

Joy in the Bible

In the summer of 2015, I had an incredible opportunity to play baseball in Europe. I played baseball for a small Christian college in Indiana, and one of my coaches had connections to several mission organizations in Europe that use baseball to share the gospel. How cool is that! I definitely thoughts so. My coach put me in contact with the missionaries, and I was set to join them in the summer. For three weeks, we traveled to Budapest, Hungry; Vienna, Austria; and Prague, Czech Republic, playing teams from all over Europe and running camps for kids. Baseball was played, and the gospel was shared. It was a life-changing experience. Leading up to the trip, I was very excited to go, but I was not excited about what it would take for me to get there. This was the first time I had ever traveled by myself. Why not make the first time international, right?

My solo journey started with a 10-hour flight from Houston, Texas, to Frankfurt, Germany. Several seasoned travelers told me to try to sleep as much as possible. That was my strategy until I found out my seating arrangement. I was in the middle seat, sitting next to a very large man. My computer wants to auto-correct "very large" with gigantic, but I don't want to be mean. I'm just stating the facts. He made his presence known and established his territory, which meant I could not move, like being in an MRI machine. Am I claustrophobic? For that flight, I was. To add to it, he loved some adult beverages. Let's just say he was sleeping like a baby by the time we were over the Atlantic. I guess his friends gave him different advice. Everyone has their own ways of coping. For me, since I couldn't sleep, movies saved the day. I remember watching Interstellar. It was the last movie I watched before we landed. Who doesn't like Matthew McConaughey? As soon as the wheels hit the ground, I was so relieved. Finally! The first step of the trip was completed. Alright, Alright, Alright.

I had a connecting flight from Frankfurt to Budapest, Hungry. I had a little bit of a layover to get through customs and then head to my next gate. Customs was jammed with people, so it took a lot of time. Once I passed through, I went to the gate that was on my ticket. When I got there, Budapest was not on the screen. I realized that my gate had been changed. I started to worry at this point. This was a huge airport that had several terminals. *Will I make my flight on time?* I found the gigantic board with all the flights to find where I needed to go. I felt like I had a good idea, so I went on my way. The longer I walked, the less confident I became. After thirty minutes of wandering, I realized that I was lost. At this point, panic started setting in. *I'm going to miss my flight. I'm going to be stuck in this airport. My luggage is going to go to Budapest, and someone's going to steal it* (silly, right?). I was visibly distraught. *What am I going to do?*

While I was losing it, a kind airport employee approached me. He spoke English, which I was incredibly grateful for since I didn't know any German. He said, "Can I help you with something?" I told him I was lost and needed help finding my gate. He said, "Let's go take a look." We walked over to one of the computer kiosks, and he looked up my flight and found my gate. What he said next was the most comforting thing I could have been told in that situation. He said, "Here, I'll just walk with you." My fear and anxiety were replaced with peace and confidence. I'm in this foreign airport where I have no idea where to go, but this man knows the airport backward and forwards, knows exactly where I need to go, and is going to help me get there. And he did, with plenty of time to spare. I thanked him over and over again for his kindness and help. His response was, "It's my job, and it's my *joy*."

Many of us feel lost, especially in our pursuit of joy. Scripture says that in this world, we are strangers and foreigners (1 Peter 2:9-12), trying to follow Jesus till it's time to go home to Heaven. But Jesus has given us the Helper, the Holy Spirit, whose job and His joy is to walk with us in all truth (John 16:13). The primary way He walks with us is by speaking to us through His Word. He is the divine author of the Scriptures, and it has been translated into our language so that we can understand the way to go. The Holy Spirit will be our guide all throughout our pursuit of joy. So, with that being said, let's begin with the Bible.

OVERVIEW OF JOY

If you are looking for joy, I promise you will find it in the Bible. You will read stories of triumph, poetic Psalms of praise, and words of encouragement to suffering people, all using the word *joy*. Joy occurs in 44 of the 66 books, with some mentioning it more than others. For example, joy will appear on every page while reading the Psalms. In the letter to the Philippians, it's almost every paragraph! In total, joy is used nearly 650 times throughout the Bible.[14]

Samah is the primary Hebrew word for joy in the Old Testament. Its verb form is translated as "to be glad or rejoice"; its noun form is "joy or gladness"; its adjective form is "joyful, glad, or merry." In all its forms, *Samah* occurs approximately 270 times in the Old Testament. Other Hebrew words for joy, such as *ranan, sus, gil,* and *alaz,* all translate "rejoice, joy, gladness" and occur a total of 215 times.[15]

Chairo is the primary Greek word for joy in the New Testament. Its verb form is translated as "rejoice or to be glad" in the majority of its occurrences; its noun form is "joy or gladness." *Chairo,* in all its forms, occurs approximately 130 times in the New Testament. Other Greek words for joy such as *agalliao, skirtao,* and *euphrosyne* all translate "rejoice, exalt, joy", occur only a combined 20 times.[16]

After identifying the different words for joy, I wanted to see how the biblical writers used them in context. As I surveyed the Bible, I found that joy's occurrences can be formed into three categories: responding in the moment, reflecting on the past, and anticipating the future. Let's begin exploring each one.

RESPONDING IN THE MOMENT

There are moments in life that can give us great joy. When a child takes their first steps. When you see the bride walking down the aisle. When you're at the table with family and friends, enjoying food and time together. Getting accepted into your dream college that you have worked so hard to get into. There are moments when joy is the natural response. I'm sure you can think of several times in your life where that has been true! When surveying the Bible, joy is also a common response to certain events and moments. I've collected a brief sampling.

Worshiping God

In the Old Testament, the place of worship was the Tabernacle or the Temple. Before your favorite worship band and hymn writer existed, there was David and the Sons of Korah. They were the first worship leaders to write prayers and worship songs, which comprise most of the Psalms. Psalm 16:11 says, "In your presence there is fullness of *joy*; at your right hand are pleasures forevermore," and Psalm 21:6 says, "You make him glad with the *joy* of your presence." In both Psalms, the worshipper responds to God's presence. The Hebrew word for presence is *panach*, which literally means "face." This is a Hebrew word picture of the Psalmist being face-to-face with God as if having a one-on-one moment with Him. This intimate time with God results in fullness of joy and gladness. The worshipper doesn't have joy because of what God has done but simply because of who He is. God is the object of their joy. His presence leads to rejoicing, praising, and singing (Psalm 84:2).

God's Word
When Israel returned from Jerusalem after their exile, Ezra, the priest, gathered the people in the city to teach them the Torah for seven straight days. I've been a part of long Bible lessons before, but not that long! After the seven days of teaching God's Word, the people's initial response was weeping and mourning over their sins because they thought they were going to die. But Ezra and the priests told the people to stop mourning and instead have joy! Ezra told the people, "Do not be grieved, for the *joy* of the Lord is your strength" (Nehemiah 8:10). The Hebrew word for strength is *moaz*, which is also translated as "refuge or safe place." In other words, don't be sad or afraid because of your sin, but the joy of the Lord is your safe place. They were convicted of how evil they were but quickly rejoiced by how good God's mercy and grace are. Because the Israelites understood the Word and its good news, they rejoiced (Nehemiah 8:12)! Today, there is joy for those who delight in the Word as well (Psalm 119:111)!

God's Provision
Most of these occurrences involve God providing bountiful wealth and harvest for His people (Deuteronomy 12:7, 16:5). Their joy was in God for providing for their needs. Also, there was joy in enjoying God's provision. Solomon wrote in Ecclesiastes, "And I commend *joy*, for man has nothing better under the sun but to eat and drink and be *joyful*," and later, "Go, eat your bread with *joy*, and drink your wine with a merry heart, for God has already approved what you do" (Eccl. 8:15, 9:7). Now reading this, you might think Solomon is condoning self-indulgence. That is not the case. Solomon tested that experiment on his own, and it cost

him greatly. Solomon says that God has provided us with good things to enjoy but within His will. It is good to enjoy food and drinks as long as we don't sin. God created a world for us to have joy in, but only if we stay within His loving boundaries.

Serving God

There is a story in Luke 10 where Jesus sent out seventy-two of His followers to perform miracles in towns. After casting out demons, Luke says, "The seventy-two returned with *joy*, saying, 'Lord, even the demons are subject to us in your name!'" (Luke 10:17) When the followers returned, they were overjoyed by how Jesus used them and wanted to tell Him all about it. Think about a time when God used you. Wasn't it exciting and fulfilling, and you were eager to tell others about it? That is the experience these followers had. As Jesus responded to their joy, He also promised they would have joy in the future. Jesus said, "Do not *rejoice* in this, that the spirits are subject to you, but *rejoice* that your names are written in heaven." (Luke 10:20). In other words, the joy we experience now in serving the Lord is no comparison to the joy we will experience in Heaven. One day, all faithful followers of Jesus will hear Him say, "Well done, good and faithful servant…enter into the *joy* of your master" (Matthew 25:23). Not only will we have joy, but Jesus will too, and that is the best joy in heaven and earth!

Fellowship with God's People

In the closing of his letter to the Romans, Paul expressed his yearning to meet them and asked for their prayers "so that by God's will I may come to you with *joy* and be refreshed in your company" (Romans 15:32). John wrote something similar to close out his second letter. He wrote, "Though I have much to write to you, I would rather not use paper and ink. Instead, I hope to come to you and talk face to face, so that our *joy* may be complete" (2 John 12). I love what Tony Reinke says about this verse. He says, "John used technology to communicate, but he knew that his letter was only part of communication…face-to-face fellowship had to follow."[17] Technology has changed significantly since the first century, considering we primarily communicate with our thumbs instead of pen and papyrus. But what hasn't changed is our need for face-to-face fellowship with other believers. Only in those moments can we experience joy to its fullness.

Suffering for God

When Israel was experiencing famine and was on the verge of exile, the prophet Habakkuk exclaimed, "Yet I will *rejoice* in the Lord;   I will take *joy* in the God of my salvation" (Habakkuk 3:18). In Acts 5, the Apostles were imprisoned, beaten, and threatened to not speak about Jesus in public. How did they respond? "They left the presence of the council, *rejoicing* that they were counted worthy to suffer dishonor for the name" (Acts 5:41). This wasn't just an isolated event. The apostles wrote extensively about their joy despite suffering for their faith. Most notable is Paul's letter to the Philippians. In its short four chapters, he mentions joy sixteen times while in a Roman prison awaiting his potential execution. But Paul didn't just talk about his joy; he also commanded it. "*Rejoice* in the Lord always; again I will say, *rejoice!*" (Philippians 4:4). The other apostles command it as well (James 1:2-4, 1 Peter 1:6-9). In many of these occurrences, the reason for the apostle's joy is because they believed their suffering served a great purpose of producing and proving one's faith. That's why they didn't resist suffering; they rejoiced in it!

Suffering is part of all of our stories, and we want to know how to have joy in our suffering as well. This is so important, that I dedicated a whole chapter to bring clarity and practicality to it. Hang in there. It'll be worth it.

God's Gospel

You've probably read these passages if you have ever done Advent with your family during Christmas. In Luke 2, after Jesus was born in Bethlehem, an angel appeared to shepherds in a field and said, "Fear not, for behold, I bring you good news of great *joy* that will be for all the people" (Luke 2:10). The Magi "*rejoiced* exceedingly with great *joy*" when they saw the star that would lead them to Jesus (Matthew 2:10). The long-awaited Savior of the world had arrived, and that gave people joy. Jesus' arrival was certainly good news, but what He came to do brought even greater joy. His death and resurrection for the forgiveness of sins became the gospel message that the apostles were commissioned to preach. The gospel was not received by all, but when it was received, it was received with joy. When Philip shared the gospel with Samaritans, "there was so much *joy* in that city" (Acts 8:8). We love hearing good news, and we love giving good news, and sharing Jesus is the best news. Think back to when you received the gospel and the joy it brought you! That leads to our next section.

REFLECTING ON THE PAST

A while back, Samantha and I were going through storage bins from our attic. While working through the mountain of bins, we came across some from our childhood. They were full of items from our childhood bedrooms, such as posters, books, toys, and even our trophies! The difference between Samantha's and my trophies was that she won at sports; mine were participation trophies. She had one from winning a regional gymnastics meet; I had one from playing t-ball. Now, we both ended up playing sports in college, where we met, so it all worked out, I guess.

As we looked through these bins, we found ourselves slowing down and reflecting. It brought back memories and prompted stories to share. At that moment, we had joy reflecting on what God had done in our lives. Similarly, there are many places where the biblical authors reflect on God's work in the past, which leads to an expression of joy. The common theme of these occurrences centers around God's deliverance. Specifically, the writers reflect on God delivering His people from their enemies, sorrow, and sin.

Deliverance from Enemies

These occurrences are times of joyful celebration (2 Chronicles 20:27, 1 Samuel 18:6)! The most notable deliverance in Israel's history was the Exodus from Egypt. After enduring 400 years of unjust slavery, God used Moses to deliver His people by sending ten plagues on Eygpt and then parted the Red Sea for Israel to escape. This was an event worth remembering! God certainly thought so. As He prepared the Jews for the Exodus, God commanded His people to have a yearly Passover feast to remember and celebrate God saving Israel (Exodus 12:1-30). To this day, Jews take off work, gather with family and friends, eat delicious food, play games, read Scripture, pray, and sing songs to celebrate what God did.

Recently, I participated in my first Passover seder with some of my Messianic Jewish friends. One of the things we did was sing the *Hallel*, which is Hebrew for "praise." Hallel is a Jewish liturgy made up of Psalms 113-118, often called the "Egyptian Hallel. These songs were written about the events of the Exodus and are sung at every Passover to remember and celebrate. Psalm 118 is the last song of the Hallel, and it says, "out of my distress I called on the Lord;   the Lord answered me and set me free" and "this is the day that the Lord has made; let us *rejoice* and be glad in it" (Ps. 118:5, 24).

I learned from this experience that Jews know how to party. But it's not partying for the sake of partying; they party with purpose! They celebrate the Passover and the other feasts and festivals instituted by the Lord to regularly remember and reflect what He has done for them (Lev. 23). I learned that God doesn't want joy to be just a response; He wants joy to be a rhythm of remembering.

Deliverance From Sorrow

In the Old Testament, mourning and sorrow often contrast with joy and gladness. You may have heard Psalm 30:5, "weeping may tarry for the night, but *joy* comes with the morning." In Jewish theology, sorrow and joy are not experienced simultaneously, but God replaces sorrow with joy. An example of this is when a loved one dies. In Jewish tradition, when a loved one dies, a "mourning period" is commissioned.

For seven days, family and friends will remain in one home to weep, pray, and read Scripture. Sometimes, professional mourners are hired to comfort and cry with the family. That's still a service available today!

The point of this is to take time to grieve intentionally. As Solomon said, there is a time to mourn and a time to have joy (Eccl. 3:4). It's not to say that they'll be done grieving and full of joy after the seven days. Rather, it begins the journey back to joy, which requires them to work through sorrow, not avoid it. When we trust God, He is faithful in replacing our sorrow with joy in due time. There will come a point when we get to the other side of our sorrow, reflect on God's hand of redemption, and have joy for what He has done. Redeeming is what God does best, and He has joy in doing it (Zeph. 3:17).

This concept is also found in the New Testament. One time, Jesus spoke to His disciples about His impending death and said to them, "You will be sorrowful, but your sorrow will turn into *joy*...you have sorrow now, but I will see you again, and your hearts will *rejoice*, and no one will take your *joy* from you" (John 16:20, 22). Jesus knew He would die and resurrect, but He also knew how His disciples would feel. While Jesus was on earth, He experienced sorrow and joy. Jesus grieved when he saw his friend Lazarus dead, and He wept (John 11:35). Jesus was called "a man of sorrows" for the death He would endure on the cross for our sins (Isaiah 53:3), but with the joy set before Him, he endured the cross (Hebrews 12:2).

Jesus knew His death was going to be traumatizing for His disciples, but He knew the joy they would have when they saw Him alive. For the rest of their lives, they will have joy reflecting on Jesus' resurrection and enjoy sharing it with others to the ends of the earth. This joy is so deep that even Christians can endure sorrow and be full of joy (2 Corinthians 7:4). Nevertheless, living in sorrow is hard, but we're not alone. Jesus is with us in our sorrow, and so are others. As Paul says, "*Rejoice* with those who *rejoice*, weep with those who weep" (Romans 12:15). Pursuing joy is not a solo journey but one with the Lord and His people.

Deliverance From Sins

Since the Garden of Eden, humans have sinned against God, separating us from Him. But God, in His love, put in place a redemptive plan to rescue us from our sins and redeem us back to Himself. God chose Israel to work out His plan by revealing Himself to them and giving them the Law. By putting their faith in God and following the Law, Israel could be in right relationship with Him. Reflecting on this, Psalm 71 says, "My lips shout for *joy*, when I sing praises to you; my soul also, which you have redeemed." Isaiah said, "I will greatly *rejoice* in the Lord; my soul shall exult in my God, for he has clothed me with the garments of salvation" (Isaiah 61:10).

But Israel was unfaithful and couldn't keep the Law. But the Law wasn't the solution; it was a setup for the Savior. God sent Jesus, the Son of God, to live the perfect life under the Law that we could never live and paid the penalty for our sins on the cross. He rose from the dead in victory, offering forgiveness of sins and eternal life for whoever trusts in Him. That is good news worth rejoicing! Paul certainly thought so when he wrote Romans 5:11, which says, "We also *rejoice* in God through our Lord Jesus Christ, through whom we have now received reconciliation."

The broken relationship with God is now restored through Jesus. Reflecting on how Jesus saved us should give us joy!

When I was twelve years old, I didn't like going to church. Getting up early, dressing nice, singing songs, and listening to a message wasn't appealing to me. I was also in the 5-6 grade ministry, which is awkward for everyone involved, so I avoided that at all costs. I was the kid who stayed in the adult service, drawing monkeys firing cannon balls on the bulletin, and just trying to pass the time until lunch. Typically, I would tune out the pastor's message, focusing on my bulletin artwork, but one Sunday morning was different. The pastor shared the gospel plainly, and the Holy Spirit captivated my attention. For the first time, I felt deep conviction for my sin. I couldn't stop thinking about it all day. That night, in my bedroom, I asked Jesus to save me, and I surrendered my life to Him. That day, Jesus changed my life. Reflecting on how Jesus saved me brings great joy, and I know it brings Him joy too (Luke 15:5-7)! I was dead and now am alive; I was lost but now am found (Luke 15:24).

How about you? Does Christ saving you bring you joy? Often, we forget what Christ has done for us. Echoing David, maybe we should ask the Lord to "restore to me the *joy* of your salvation" (Psalm 51:12). There is joy to be had for what Christ has saved us from, but there's also joy in what is to come.

ANTICIPATING THE FUTURE

A few months ago, we welcomed our second child, Ethan (aka E-Money), into the world.

Although we were so excited for his arrival, the weeks leading up to his due date were agonizing.

If there were any signs of contractions, we were ready to go. We definitely had some false start penalties on the field. Braxton Hicks is the worst. Anytime I got a text or call notification from Samantha, my heart would race. I would answer, "Is it time??" It was never time. After three weeks of eager anticipation, Sam went into labor on her due date (which only happens in 4% of pregnancies), and we met E-Money at 2 am that night. We were overwhelmed with joy when we held him in our arms and finally saw him face-to-face. Everything we had been through was worth it!

In a similar way, the New Testament writers had an eager anticipation to be reunited with Jesus. At any moment, whether through death or Jesus' glorious return, they could see their Savior face-to-face again. Anticipating the future brought them great joy.

Hope and Joy

In the New Testament, there is a relationship between hope and joy. Paul makes this connection throughout the book of Romans. He wrote, "Through him [Jesus] we have also obtained access by faith into this grace in which we stand, and we *rejoice* in hope of the glory of God" (Romans 5:2). Then later in the letter, he commands, "*Rejoice* in hope" (Romans 12:12). Peter wrote in his letter, "he [Jesus] has caused us to be born again to a living hope through the resurrection of Jesus Christ from the dead, to an inheritance that is imperishable, undefiled, and unfading, kept in heaven for you...In this you *rejoice*." (1 Peter 1:3,4,6). This is just a sampling of many occurrences where hope and joy are found together. So, what is the relationship between hope and joy? First, we must define hope.

When the New Testament writers used the word hope, they used it differently than the way we use it today. When we use hope, it has a sense of wishful thinking and uncertainty. "I hope I get the job." "I hope my team wins." "I hope my test results come back normal." This kind of hope desires something good to happen in the future but isn't sure it will happen. Today's hope is uncertain, but New Testament hope is certain. New Testament hope is the confident expectations for future events.[18] An everyday example of this kind of hope is our confidence that the sun will rise tomorrow morning. No one says with uncertainty, "I hope the sun will rise tomorrow." Why? Because we've seen the sun rise throughout our life without fail. It would be very concerning if it didn't!

Just like we have a confident expectation for the sun to rise, the apostles had a confident expectation for the Son to return. Why? Because just like the sun, they were witnesses of Jesus' faithfulness. He consistently did what He said He would do without fail. If He was faithful to keep His promises in the past, He is faithful to keep His promises in the future. Even if they died before His return, they lived by the mantra "to live is Christ, and to die is gain" (Phil. 1:21). They believed no matter what happened to them, they would reunite with Jesus in heaven and receive their promises. What promises did they hope for, which we can hope for as well?

Hope for Eternal Life

This promise is the cornerstone of the Christian faith, that whoever believes in Jesus will not perish but have eternal life (John 3:16). For the apostles, eternity was their priority.

Paul wrote, "We look not to the things that are seen but to the things that are unseen. For the things that are seen are transient, but the things that are unseen are eternal" (1 Cor. 4:17-18). Eternity influenced how they served, spent money, worked, and shared the gospel. They lived not to store up treasure on earth but to store up their treasure in heaven (Matthew 6:19-21). Peter says this treasure is "an inheritance that is imperishable, undefiled, and unfading, kept in heaven for you" (1 Peter 1:4). There are no stock market crashes or diminishing returns in heaven. Our reward is secure and waiting for us there.

In addition, the hope for eternity was the apostle's primary motivation for enduring suffering. Jesus told his disciples that when they would suffer for His name, they should "*rejoice in that day, and leap for joy*, for behold, your reward is great in heaven" (Luke 6:23). The apostles believed this promise, and it gave them hope in their suffering. Paul said, "Yes, and I will *rejoice*...as it is my eager expectation and hope that I will not be at all ashamed, but with full courage now as always Christ will be honored in my body, whether by life or by death" (Philippians 1:18, 20). We can endure pain and suffering because we have something to look forward to. Not just something, *everything.*

We will experience persecution, physical suffering, or loss in this life, but we can endure because of the hope we have in Christ. Even for loved ones who have gone ahead to be with Jesus, we have hope and joy that we will be reunited with them again. But Jesus doesn't just promise us eternal life; He also promises to bring us into his family.

Hope for Spiritual Adoption

Paul highlights this adoption in Galatians 4:4-7 and twice in Romans 8. In the middle of Romans 8, Paul writes that believers "have the first fruits of the Spirit" (Romans 8:23a). What are these first fruits of the Spirit? Don't be confused with the fruit of the Spirit in Galatians 5. Paul is highlighting something else. In Romans 8, Paul uses an agricultural practice from the day to illustrate a spiritual reality. The first fruits were the first fruits to sprout from the vine. A vinedresser would tend their vineyard every day, eagerly anticipating the first fruits of the vine to sprout. Once sprouted, the vinedresser would eat the grape or olive, giving them a taste of the harvest to come.

Similarly, the Spirit gives believers the first fruits of heaven. While here on earth, He gives us hope for what is to come. One of those first fruits is our spiritual adoption. Concerning our spiritual adoption, Paul wrote in Romans 8:15, "The Spirit you received does not make you slaves so that you live in fear again; rather, the Spirit you received brought about your adoption to sonship. And by him we cry, *"Abba,* Father." Later, Paul wrote that believers "groan inwardly as we wait eagerly for adoption as sons" (Romans 8:23). What's interesting about these two verses is that the tense changes. Verse 15 is in the past completed tense as if the adoption is final, but verse 23 is written as if we're waiting for the adoption to happen in the future. Putting these verses together can be confusing. Aren't we already adopted? What are we eagerly waiting for?

To go home.

Like any adoption, there is a process. Usually, the parents meet with the child, build a relationship, review the legal documentation, and pay the adoption fees. However, the adoption isn't complete until the parents take the child home. For us, the Father has chosen us (Eph. 1:4, 1 Peter 2:9), Jesus has paid with His blood the right to become children of God (John 1:12), and the Spirit has secured us (2 Cor. 1:22, Rom. 8:16). Today, we are in an anticipation period waiting for the day for our Father to take us home. In the meantime, as we wait, we have time to build our relationship with our Father. That's the first fruit! Through the Spirit, we can commune with God day by day, moment by moment, step by step. He knows everything about us, and we have every opportunity to get to know Him. We can come to Him for anything and everything. He wants us to! He takes good care of His children. Then, one day, we will see Him face-to-face, and oh, what a joyful time that will be!

Hope for Redeemed Bodies

In Romans 8, Paul expresses that the world, believers, and the Spirit are "groaning" (Rom. 8:22, 23, 26). These are not the groans you hear in the back seat asking, "Are we there yet?" or the groans you make getting out of bed in the morning. These are groans of deep pain. Paul describes this pain as childbirth (Rom. 8:22). As I opened this section, I recalled E-Money's birth story. But as I did, I highlighted the anticipation and joy, but I didn't highlight the pain. Personally, I have never experienced labor pains, but I have witnessed it twice. It is an excruciating experience, to say the least. This is the picture Paul chose to depict the pain we experience in our broken bodies, and we are more than aware. We are plagued with all kinds of diseases, disorders, and disasters that cause our bodies pain. We have the virus of sin coursing through us, which causes destruction to ourselves and others. Nothing is the way it should be, and we are groaning because of it. But, just like labor pain, something new is coming, which should give us hope and joy.

Jesus will turn our groaning into glory when He makes all things new (Rev. 21:5). There will be a day when there will be no more cancer, autoimmune disorders, mental illness, miscarriages, blindness, or paralysis. We will have glorified bodies with no weaknesses, limitations, or pain. Just as Jesus died and rose with a glorified body, so will we rise with our glorified bodies (Romans 6:5). Everything will be perfect, and you will be more alive than ever before. In her book *Heaven: Your Real Home,* Joni Eareckson Tada wrote, "Somewhere in my broken, paralyzed body is the seed of what I shall become. The paralysis makes what I am to become all the more grand when you contrast atrophied, useless legs against splendorous resurrected legs. I'm convinced that if there are mirrors in heaven (and why not?), the image I'll see will be unmistakably 'Joni,' although a much better, brighter Joni."[19] That kind of incredible hope is what believers have to look forward to in heaven.

So, how does all this hope relate to joy? John Piper offers an illustration I find helpful, which he calls "The Hope Tree." Now imagine hope is a tree. The soil from which hope grows is faith in Jesus and the richness of God's grace. When the seed is planted, it eventually sprouts (born again), and so hope begins. The nutrients that help hope grow are the promises of God's Word (eternal life, spiritual adoption, and redemption of bodies). The question is: does this tree bear fruit? The answer from the

New Testament writers is yes! The fruit is *joy*.[20] In other words, our hope in Jesus produces joy within us.

You see, hope gives us an eager expectation for our eternal future. No matter how good or bad life gets, we know the best is yet to come. Like a laboring mother who endures excruciating pain in order to embrace her child, so we will endure our pain knowing we will embrace our Savior one day (John 16:21). Our hope and joy are just a taste of what is to come. I like the Christian Standard Bible rendering of Romans 5:5a, "This hope will not disappoint us" (CSB). Have you ever been disappointed? Someone may have let you down. Maybe your expectations were not met. Someone over-promised and under-delivered. That won't be the case with Jesus. Not one person who gets to heaven will feel gypped. On the contrary, we will be the most alive we have ever been and feel the most intense joy we have ever experienced. We will finally be home with Jesus, who will be overjoyed to have us with Him forever. No more groaning, only glory.

CONCLUSION

This chapter may have felt like drinking from a fire hose, and I totally understand. My goal was to present the most comprehensive use of joy in the Bible. Candidly, what I shared with you is just scratching the surface of the 650 occurrences. If there's a particular verse that you didn't see listed, don't worry—there is more to come. But this lays a strong foundation for the remainder of the book.

The common pattern of joy in the Bible is that God's people express their joy in response to who God is, what he has done for them in the past and present, and what He will do for them in the future. God is the object and the source of their joy, but they are the object of God's joy as well. There is also joy in being in fellowship with God's people through eating, celebrating, and serving. Even in sorrow and suffering, there is joy in being together and hope for the future. Rejoicing is a victory cry over enemies and over death itself. Overall, joy isn't just a response to good things; it's a response to God's goodness.

As you continue your pursuit of joy, my prayer for you is this: "May the God of hope fill you with all joy and peace in believing, so that by the power of the Holy Spirit you may abound in hope" (Romans 15:13).

REFLECTION AND DISCUSSION QUESTIONS

1. Of the things in this chapter (Worshiping God, God's Word, God's Provision, Serving God, Fellowship with God's People, Suffering for God, God's Gospel), which one would you say you experience the most joy?
2. What do you think Paul means, "Rejoice in the Lord always, I'll say it again rejoice" (Philippians 4:4)?
3. What's been your experience with sorrow and suffering? Were you able to have joy in it?
4. How did you come to faith? Take some time to reflect and share (if applicable).
5. What do you think fellowship with others has to do with joy?
6. Why do you think hope and joy are closely related?

CHAPTER THREE
Joy in Psychology

"**D**addy, will you watch *Inside Out* with me?" This was probably the hundredth time Ellie had asked me this. *Inside Out* is her favorite movie by far, and honestly, it's one of my favorites, too! If you haven't seen it, this is my courteous spoiler alert and my encouragement to see it, even if you are a well-to-do adult with no young children. Go live a little! By the time this book is out, *Inside Out* Two will be released. For clarification, I will be referencing the first *Inside Out* movie. Oh, and go see that one too. So good.

If you don't know, *Inside Out* is a Disney Pixar animated comedy that portrays a young girl named Riley. She is an 11-year-old child who lives with her parents in Minnesota. All is good in the world until her father gets a new job in San Francisco, and the whole family is uprooted and relocated. This move across the country deeply affects Riley, which acts as the backdrop for the movie. What's interesting is the movie doesn't portray Riley as the main character, but rather, she's the setting. The movie takes place inside Riley's mind, and her emotions are the main characters.

Disney personalized these emotions as distinct beings living in Riley's mind called "the Headquarters" (clever wordplay). These emotions include Fear, Anger, Disgust, Sadness, and *Joy*. Each of these emotions tries to help Riley navigate life but finds themselves in a crisis when Riley's family moves across the country. Joy is portrayed as the leader and tries to keep Riley "happy," even though there is little to be happy about. Unfortunately, Sadness takes over Riley's mind, which drives her into isolation and depression. All of Riley's emotional connections, memories, and interests start to fade away. Anger, Fear, and Disgust want to help, but they only make things worse. It was up to Joy to save the day. Through a theatrical journey through Riley's mind, Joy ultimately helps Sadness and the other emotions bring balance back to Riley's mind and wellness to her life. Joy indeed saved the day!

Inside Out is a fun movie aimed to bring clarity to emotional health in children. Watching it for the hundredth time with Ellie stirred my curiosity about how psychology views joy. So, I began researching, starting with *Inside Out*. Does *Inside Out* accurately depict human emotions, and do they accurately depict what joy is? Pixar, concerning the character joy, stated:

> "Joy's goal has always been to make sure Riley stays happy. She is lighthearted, optimistic, and determined to find the fun in every situation. Joy sees challenges in Riley's life as opportunities

and the less happy moments as hiccups on the way back to something great. As long as Riley is happy, so is Joy."[21]

Is that true? Is joy an emotion that tries to make us optimistic, have fun, and be happy? You might think, "It's a Pixar movie; it's not trying to be accurate." But actually, Pixar was trying to be accurate.

PSYCHOLOGY'S VIEW OF JOY

In a Psychology Today article titled "Inside Out: Emotional Truth by Way of Pixar," Dr. Janina Scarlet writes, "What's really powerful about this film is how accurate it is to cognitive, developmental, and clinical psychology. The five emotions used in this film are, in fact, five of the six scientifically validated universal emotions (the 6th one being surprise)."[22] Even though we don't have animated characters running around in our heads (I find that disappointing), the movie does depict what psychology believes are the five basic human emotions: Fear, Anger, Disgust, Sadness, and *Joy*.

In her article, Dr. Scarlett mentioned the work of Dr. Paul Ekman, who served as a scientific advisor for Pixar in creating *Inside Out*. Dr. Ekman has studied human emotions since the early 1960s. TIME Magazine named Dr. Ekman as one of the 100 most influential people in the world and is the fifteenth most influential psychologist of the twenty-first century.[23] Through a half-century of research, Ekman helped name the five basic human emotions. Interestingly, the names for the five emotions have stayed the same over the years except for one. *Joy*.

In 2007, Dr. Ekman's book *Emotion Revealed* lists "happiness."[24] In 2015, "joy" is portrayed in the movie *Inside Out*. In 2016, Dr. Ekman and his daughter, Dr. Eve Ekman, created "The Atlas of Emotions," which lists "enjoyment."[25] So why has Anger, Disgust, Sadness, and Fear remained the same, but there's been a rewording for joy within the last 20 years?

Dr. Ekman's rewording of joy exemplifies how psychology has viewed joy for several decades. Overall, joy is viewed as a positive emotion interchangeable with other positive emotions like happiness, gratitude, pride, and contentment. The Oxford Companion to Emotion and the Affective Sciences defines joy as "a pleasant state that shares conceptual space with other positive emotions such as gladness, elation, happiness, and, to a lesser extent, amusement."[26]

Typically, joy is an umbrella term for your feelings after a good experience or a desirable outcome.[27] You get a promotion at your job. You meet your weight loss goal. You finish your master's degree. You finally get your toddler down for a nap. Anything you believe is good can result in joy. Good food. Good Netflix show. Good coffee. Good workout. Good hair day. Because psychology has viewed joy this way, joy has been overlooked, and very little research has been done on it. Joy is one of the last major positive emotions to be explored and has been neglected by psychologists.[28]

A major reason psychologists haven't researched joy is because of the mental health crisis. Much of psychology's attention has been researching negative emotions such as Sadness, Fear, and Anger, more specifically, disorders such as anxiety and depression. As shared in chapter one, one in three Americans showed symptoms of anxiety and depression in 2023, and nearly half of young adults. Because of this crisis, psychology has focused its research efforts on understanding these disorders and how to treat people effectively. Since this is a major problem in our day, I wanted to learn more about it. Could there be clues to finding joy?

THE MENTAL HEALTH CRISIS

Anxiety and depression are complex disorders with multiple contributing factors. Each individual's experience is unique, and a combination of biological, psychological, and environmental factors can influence the onset of these conditions. Biological factors include being genetically predisposed. Studies have shown that individuals with a family history of anxiety or depression are more likely to experience these conditions themselves.[29]

Psychological factors such as personality traits, coping mechanisms, and cognitive patterns can also contribute to anxiety and depression. People who tend to worry excessively, have low self-esteem, or struggle with negative thinking patterns are more susceptible to these conditions. Traumatic experiences such as abuse, neglect, or loss can also trigger anxiety and depression.

Environmental factors can also play a significant role in developing anxiety and depression. Stressful life events such as job loss, financial difficulties, relationship problems, or chronic illness can trigger these conditions. Social factors like isolation, lack of social support, or ongoing exposure to violence or trauma can also contribute. Also, lifestyle factors such as poor diet, lack of exercise, substance abuse, and inadequate sleep can impact mental health.

When it comes to treatment, depending on the person's cause of symptoms, a therapist will provide a personalized strategy to help clients manage their anxiety and depression. This strategy often includes Preventing, Preparing, and Persevering.

1. Prevent

Therapists help clients prevent the escalation of anxiety or depressive symptoms. They will prescribe anti-anxiety and anti-depressant medication to correct neurotransmitter imbalances. In addition, therapists commonly use talk therapy, such as Cognitive-Behavioral Therapy (CBT), to help people identify and change negative thought patterns and behaviors contributing to anxiety and depression. The goal is to restore the mind and body to an emotional balance.

2. Prepare

Therapists help clients prepare to fight against anxiety and depression symptoms. This approach is proactive instead of reactive. In a way, it's like training the mind and body for sports and physical activity. This includes regular exercise, a healthy diet, sufficient sleep, and stress management techniques. CBT and positive self-talk are also ways of training the mind for when negative thoughts and emotions try to intrude.

3. Persevere

Therapists help clients persevere through anxiety and depression symptoms. These disorders can make people feel hopeless, as if they will never overcome their struggles. Building a strong support network of friends and loved ones is often advised, as well as group therapy. It's also vital to help clients build resiliency. The idea is to help clients not to avoid certain situations that cause anxiety and depression but rather equip them to overcome them.

My Experience

Several years ago, I battled through a season of anxiety and depression. At the time, I was a full-time pastor, a full-time seminary student, and a husband and father to a toddler. A normal day for me was working nine to five, coming home and spending time with the family, starting homework around nine o'clock, and working till one to three in the morning. I did this five days a week, plus schoolwork on the weekends, for three straight years. I was exhausted and overwhelmed. To add to the stress and lack of sleep, I was also in the middle of a potential job change that would impact our whole family. To put a cherry on top, I was also diagnosed with an auto-immune disease during this time, where I no longer could eat gluten or dairy (I miss queso so much). While going through all this, I remember taking a stress test called the Holmes-Rahe Life Stress Inventory. The average person should score under 150, which means you have a healthy amount of stress in your life. Anything over 300 means you have an 80% chance of having a mental breakdown. I scored a 450. Turns out it was right. I did have a mental breakdown.

One Sunday morning, I was responsible for making the announcements for our church service. Usually, I would get anxious before going on stage, but nothing abnormal. At this point, I had preached and made announcements for five years, so I was in familiar territory. Well, as I was making announcements in the second service, I felt my heart race, my throat swelled shut, I struggled to breathe, I couldn't speak, and my body was shaking uncontrollably. I had a full-blown panic attack on stage in front of 450 people. I literally heard gasps in the crowd. I was so embarrassed and felt so much shame. I ran off the stage straight to my car and cried alone. *Am I going to lose my job? What are people thinking right now? How will I ever be able to show my face at church again?*

The next day, I snuck into my office and tried to hide. But I couldn't hide for long. Our Executive Pastor came over and asked if he could meet with me. In my mind, I was thinking, *"That's it. They're going to let me go."* That couldn't be farther from the truth. As I sat across from him, he told me how much I was loved and how much the church wanted to care for me. He told me the church leadership was willing to put me through therapy so I could get the help I needed. In that moment, I felt relief, safe, and loved. I agreed to go to therapy, and I spent a combination of a year with two excellent Christian therapists who cared for me well.

In therapy, we went through the three P's. My therapist helped me understand that I needed to renew a lot of my thinking because I was believing lies that weren't true (Romans 12:2, 2 Corinthians 10:5). For example, I believed my performance determined people's acceptance of me. If I didn't perform well, then people would reject me. If I performed well, people would accept me. This thinking was traced back to when I played baseball as a child and even through college. My therapist reminded me that in Christ, my performance doesn't determine His acceptance. Jesus loves me and accepts me for who I am as His child, and that is what matters most (Romans 8:38-39). What a freeing truth!

In addition to this change in thinking, I also made some lifestyle adjustments. I started going to bed consistently at a good time, taking days off from homework, and eating healthier. My therapist also gave me breathing techniques and self-talk practices to help me during an anxiety episode. After some time and hard work, I felt like I was in a healthier place physically, spiritually, and emotionally. I was grateful for the godly men who helped me through that dark time. But even though I felt like I could manage my anxiety and depression, I felt like something else was still missing. Even though my negative emotions were more under control, I still didn't have a consistent joy like I thought I would.

I thought preventing, preparing, and persevering through my anxiety and depression would free me to have the joyful life I've always wanted, but that wasn't the case. *What's wrong with me?* That bothered me for a long time, but I continued on with life. It wasn't until I started researching for this book that I came across someone who may have the answer. In fact, this person offers a different approach to the problem of anxiety and depression. Maybe the solution isn't just about preventing, preparing, and persevering through anxiety and depression, but it's also about *pursuing* joy.

PURSUING JOY

Not too long ago, I had the pleasure of meeting Dr. Philip Watkins. He is a recently retired psychology professor and researcher from Eastern Washington University. Dr. Watkins spent the first ten years of his career researching depression but later found a passion for researching positive psychology, such as gratitude and joy. Due to his research, he and his colleagues are considered experts in the study of joy.

As I said before, psychology has not researched joy because it's generally believed to be synonymous with other positive emotions. But that is what fueled Dr. Watkins and his colleague's curiosity. Is joy a distinct emotion? Dr. Watkins is the first to tell you he was a skeptic, thinking joy was like happiness and gratitude. But the research convinced him otherwise. In his own words, "I've been converted."[30]

In 2019, the Journal of Positive Psychology published Dr. Watkin's research article "Appraising Joy." Dr. Watkins and his team conducted seven research studies to determine what joy is. Their research discovered that joy is indeed unique from other positive emotions, not an umbrella term at all. They concluded that joy is distinct because it is fundamentally about *connection*.[31] Dr. Robert Emmons, Professor of Psychology at the University of California-Davis, contributed to the project. In an interview, Dr. Emmons said we can only experience joy in a relationship with someone or something that transcends ourselves: relationships with others or with a higher being.[32] What does that sound like?

Joy is about Connection

The research showed this type of connection is best explained as a *reunion*. Not your dysfunctional family reunions or your awkward class reunions. However, both of those could be entertaining! The reunion described in the research is a deep relational bond. For example, it's like being reunited with a loved one who has been serving overseas. Or you see a childhood friend that you haven't seen in years. Or when you walk through the door and you hear, "Daddy! Daddy!" All of those examples are types of reunions. The study found that the longer the person has been waiting for the reunion, the stronger the joy response.[33] That's why seeing a loved one you haven't seen in years is a more intense joy than coming home after a day's work. Nonetheless, joy is experienced. Joy is all about connection.

Joy in Psychology

Dr. Watkins told me the best picture of this in Scripture is the Prodigal Son in Luke 15:11-32. After the son rejects his father and squanders his inheritance, he shamefully comes home. But the reunion with his father wasn't full of shame and anger, but joy! The Father is full of joy seeing his son returning home alive, and he blesses him with gifts and a party. That is a picture of joy. But it's not just the Prodigal Son. Consider all the times joy is used in the Bible. Almost all of them have to do with some type of relationship, redemption, or reunion. When God's people worshiped together in the sanctuary, they had joy. When they met with God in the Scriptures, they had joy. When the apostles reunited in fellowship with other believers, their joy was complete. The apostles even had joy because of the anticipated reunion with Jesus. Also, Heaven rejoices when a lost person comes to faith and is reunited with their Creator. Joy is indeed all about connection.

So, if connection is the difference, what does that look like in everyday life? Let me give you an example using one of my favorite things in the world. Coffee! Not too long ago, I went to one of my favorite coffee shops to get an afternoon cold brew. After I ordered, I pulled around to the window to learn that the person in front of me paid for my drink! Score! I left the coffee shop feeling really good. The question is, did I experience joy? According to Dr. Watkins' research, the answer is no, but I likely experienced other positive emotions like surprise, happiness, and gratitude. I was surprised because I wasn't expecting the person's generosity (some of you hate surprises, but this was a good one!). I experienced happiness because I do enjoy delicious cold-brew coffee. I felt gratitude because a stranger paid for my coffee. But notice in this scenario I never felt connected to anyone. I never met the person; I stayed in my car; the barista gave me my coffee, and I left. It was a good feeling, but not necessarily joy.

Months later, I had another scenario nearly identical to the first, except for one difference. I went to the same coffee shop, ordered the same drink, and someone else paid for it, except this time, it wasn't a stranger; it was a friend! We both enjoy coffee and each other's company, so we decided to hang out. We had a great time! So, what's the difference between the two scenarios? The difference is connection. I may have felt surprise, happiness, and gratitude because of my friend's generosity, but I also felt joy because I was connecting with my friend. That connection will last longer than the coffee, which was much more meaningful. You can have gratitude, happiness, and other positive emotions without connection, but without connection, you can't have joy.

Joy vs Happiness

This is where many of my Christian brothers and sisters will rejoice (see what I did there) because they have been saying joy and happiness are different for years. I remember that, early on, when writing this book, I asked people to define joy for me. Almost every time I heard something like, "Well, it's not happiness." In further research, I read books and articles that said things like:

> *"Happiness is worldly, and joy is godly."*
> *"Happiness depends on circumstances, joy doesn't."*
> *"Happiness is fleeting, and joy is everlasting."*

Many believe our problem today is that we are pursuing happiness instead of joy. Or how someone else said to me, "We desire joy, but we settle for happiness." In other words, happiness is bad, and we should not pursue it. But is pursuing happiness the problem? Is happiness actually bad? As I shared in chapter one, the idea that happiness is worldly and joy is godly is not actually biblical, and some of the things we say and believe are not actually true. Yes, you read that right.

In his book titled *Happiness,* Randy Alcorn extensively builds the case for biblical happiness. He highlights that the distinction between happiness and joy is only about a hundred years old, originating sometime in the twentieth-century.[34] Before the twentieth-century, teachers, preachers, and theologians viewed joy and happiness interchangeably. For example, Charles Spurgeon (1834-1892), in a sermon titled "A Happy Christian," said, "May your Christian life be fraught with *happiness* and overflowing with *joy!*"[35] D.L. Moody (1837-1899) wrote, "All the *joys* we are to know in heaven will come from the presence of God...a *happy*-making sight."[36] Even the twentieth-century theologian and pastor A.W. Tozer (1897-1963) wrote, "The people of God ought to be the *happiest* people in all the wide world!"[37] Wait, but isn't happiness worldly? Did Tozer mean joyful?

To say happiness is not biblical is a non-biblical statement. Happiness is in the Bible and is a good thing, not bad. For example, Psalm 68:3 says, "But may the righteous be glad and rejoice before God; may they be happy and joyful" (NIV). Esther 8:16 says, "For the Jews, it was a time of happiness and joy, gladness and honor" (NIV). You see, the biblical authors at times used happiness and joy interchangeably, or they used them together to emphasize something. We do the same thing today. For example, have you ever said "small little" or "tiny little" before? Samantha says I do this all the time. I said recently, "I went to this tiny little restaurant and had some delicious tacos." Tiny and little are similar words but are used together to emphasize something. That's often how joy, happiness, gladness, cheerfulness, and delight are used in the Bible.

So why do we see joy more than happiness in the Bible? The reason is it often gets lost in translation. The words for happiness in the Hebrew and Greek are the same words for "blessing" or "blessed." Blessing in the Bible has a wide range of meanings, such as divine favor, giving or receiving of gifts, and receiving an inheritance, but it can also mean being happy. One way to think of it is that happiness is the correct response to favor, gifts, and inheritance!

One of those words in the New Testament is the word *makarios*, which Jesus used a lot. For example, He used this word when He taught the Beatitudes in Matthew 5:2-12. When Jesus was teaching the crowd what it was like to be a part of His kingdom, He told them "blessed" or "happy" are those who are poor in spirit, mourn, meek, hunger and thirst for righteousness, merciful, pure, peacemakers, and persecuted. Wait, what? Really? Jesus' audience would have been shocked because many of those things don't sound like they would make you happy! But that was Jesus' point. Things in His kingdom are backward. Everyone who heard his sermon desired blessing and happiness, but He told them it's not found in just desirable circumstances. Ultimately, happiness is found in Jesus and being in His kingdom, despite the circumstances in life. Reading this, you might think, "Wait, that sounds like joy!" Well, they are similar.

Biblically, happiness and joy are both positive emotions experienced by God's people. The distinction between the two isn't worldly versus godly; it's general versus relational. As we've learned, joy is about connection, whereas happiness doesn't require connection. For example, in the Beatitudes, Jesus promises believers will be blessed or happy by living godly. For joy, connection is necessary. Joy goes deeper because it's about love and relationships. That's not to say happiness is inferior to joy, which most people would say. They are both essential and God-given. You should never feel guilty for feeling happy. Happiness is not worldly; it's godly.

So what happened? Why do Christians view happiness so negatively? Well, in the twentieth century, when this distinction was born, consumerism took off. People started buying things not just out of need but also out of desire. Companies began to use marketing strategies to target the human heart's desire for happiness, advertising products that would make them happy. Then the mantra "do whatever makes you happy" was birthed, and happiness became the standard of life. If something makes you happy, do it. If it doesn't make you happy, don't do it. Even in relationships, you hear, "She really makes me happy!" or "I'm not happy in my marriage anymore." To sum it up, happiness is everything. And that is still very true today.

So, the twentieth-century Bible teachers responded to these messages about happiness and deemed it evil and worldly. Alcorn said that the Bible teachers "saw people trying to find happiness in sin, they concluded that pursuing happiness was sinful.[38]" So, happiness, along with joy, got lost and misunderstood for the last hundred years in the church because of an overcorrection. Happiness isn't worldly in itself, but we do pursue worldly things to try and have it. We'll cover that more in chapter five.

Also, joy is not something only exclusive to Christians. Non-believers can experience joy and happiness too, but just in a limited way. It's just like how non-believers can love but only in a limited way apart from the knowledge and experience of God's love. We were all created to have happiness and joy, but we can only experience them to the fullest by being deeply connected to God and others.

Joy Produces Flourishing

Joy is fundamental to human flourishing and well-being. For most of psychology's history, joy has been viewed as a sign of flourishing. If you have joy, you are living well, and life is good. But, research shows that joy is not just a sign of flourishing; joy produces flourishing.[39] In fact, you'll live to be healthier and live longer. Harvard University conducted a study of human development, and an IE University article summarized its findings:

> The Harvard Study of Adult Development followed a large cohort of adults and some of their descendants for 85 years, documenting a myriad of influences throughout their successes and failures. The study found that while physical health is not to be ignored, those who had strong and satisfied personal relationships were on the path to the

longest lives. As *joy* can be derived from the feeling of connection – or reconnection – with ourselves and others, the participants who felt strongly bonded with their loved ones showed greater signs of health and vitality than participants who reported having weaker relationships.[40]

So, if joy is about connection and produces flourishing, can the opposite effect be true?

Is it possible that our lack of connection with God and people is one of the contributing factors to our mental health crisis, as well as the absence of joy and flourishing? The research shows that it's more than possible.

In 2023, the Surgeon General of the United States wrote a research article titled "Our Epidemic of Loneliness and Isolation." The study found that approximately half of U.S. adults report experiencing loneliness, with some of the highest rates among young adults. The study also found that it is more dangerous to be lonely than smoking 15 cigarettes a day. Loneliness and social isolation increase the risk of premature death by 29%.[41] Not to be overdramatic, but the data shows that joy is not just a matter of mental health; it's a matter of life and death. That's why we need to get this right. We'll explore this more in the following chapters.

CONCLUSION

We started this chapter with my daughter Ellie's love for the movie Inside Out. I want you to notice the question she asked me: "Daddy, will you watch Inside Out *with me*?" This movie is her favorite, but it's not what brings her joy. What brings her joy is watching it with her daddy, and it gives her daddy joy to watch it with her, too.

Spending time with our Father gives us joy, and it gives Him joy, too. He desires to have an intimate and intentional relationship with us, and that is what our hearts desire as well. God is where we find joy, as well as relationships with others. We tend to want to do things on our own, but joy is about connection—being connected with God and connected with others.

REFLECTION AND DISCUSSION QUESTIONS

1. Out of the five basic emotions (anger, sadness, disgust, fear, and joy), what do you feel like you experience the most? What do you feel the least?
2. Have you ever experienced mental health issues? What was helpful for you?
3. Do you feel connected to God on a regular basis? Why or why not?
4. When was a time you felt intimately connected to God? (Reflect and share, if applicable)
5. Do you feel connected to people on a regular basis? Why or why not?
6. When was a time you felt intimately connected to others? (Reflect and share, if applicable.)

CHAPTER FOUR

Defining Joy

'**C**an you see anything?' Lord Carnarvon asked archeologist Howard Carter as he peered into a small opening of what seemed to be a tomb in the middle of the Egyptian desert. As Carter's eyes adjusted to the dim light, he was speechless when he saw the stunning treasure in the shadows. All Carter could say was, "Yes, it is wonderful."

I'm a sucker for a good documentary. This was a good one. For thousands of years, archeologists and grave robbers excavated the Egyptian deserts in search of the tombs of the Egyptian Pharaohs. Carter was a British archeologist consumed with Egyptology and determined to find a Pharaoh's tomb. His eyes were set on the "Valley of the Kings," which lay in Luxar, in south Egypt. There was a buzz among archeologists that royal families were buried in this valley, and discovering a Pharaoh's tomb was possible. Carter personally wanted to pursue a young teenage Pharaoh's tomb who ruled in the 1300s BC. Many archeologists had excavated the valley in search of this tomb, but to no avail. Most archeologists believed the tomb was not in the valley, so they gave up. But Carter didn't.

For nearly a decade, Carter and his team excavated the valley in search of the tomb. But year after year, there was little reward for their labor. They found ancient work huts and pottery but nothing close to a pharaoh's tomb. Carter was getting ready to give up, just like all the others.

But, in November of 1922, Carter instructed his team to dig around an area where they had worked before. On a Saturday morning, some of Carter's workers found a step underneath one of the huts, which was peculiar. After digging more, they found that this step was part of a steep staircase several feet underground. Overwhelmed with excitement, the team dug until they were met with a stone door with an 1300s BC style picture of the jackal god Anubis. Could this be what they have been looking for?

After a month of digging and delicately searching the contents of their discovery, they realized what they found was beyond anything they could have imagined. The first chamber was filled with vases, furniture, statues, jewels, chests, and a throne, all made of gold. But on the other side of the chamber was an even greater treasure. This chamber had colorful hieroglyphics on the walls and a golden box in the middle of the room. It was a tomb. But this wasn't just any tomb. This tomb belonged to none other than King Tutankhamun, otherwise known as King Tut. The young pharaoh was buried in a nest of three coffins, with the inner one made of solid gold. On the king's head laid a stunning golden portrait mask that I'm sure you have seen before in history books. Or, you can Google it! Carter's discovery was the greatest in archeological history.[42]

When Carter started his archeology journey, he wanted to find King Tut. After persistently pursuing the pharaoh for many years, he found what he was searching for. Similarly, Jesus said in Matthew 7:7-8, "Ask, and it will be given to you; seek, and you will find; knock, and it will be opened to you. For everyone who asks receives, and the one who seeks finds, and to the one who knocks it will be opened." After searching the Scriptures and extensive research, I believe the Lord has revealed what we've been looking for. Joy!

WHAT IS JOY?

Let's start here. It appears that joy is an emotion. Joy is a deep inner feeling believers have when intimately connected with God and others. Often, that deep inner feeling is outwardly expressed by praising, singing, celebrating, worshiping, dancing, crying, and laughing. When I started my research, this was not what I thought I would find. Going in, I thought joy was an attitude I could choose daily, like a holy optimism. But, the evidence is clear that joy is an emotion, and I'm not the only one who came to this conclusion.

Marianne Meye Thompson, Professor of New Testament at Fuller Theological Seminary, wrote an article titled "Reflections on Joy in the Bible." She also surveyed the use of joy in the Bible and concluded that joy "is an effusive emotional response … joy reflects God's rejoicing in the world and its goodness … the expression of gratitude and praise that flows from a resolute, trusting heart that is suffused by hope in God."[43] The Expository Dictionary of Bible Words says joy is, "the emotion of rejoicing in the general sense of feeling good ... a feeling of delight and well-being."[44] John Piper wrote, "Christian joy is not an act of willpower. It is a spontaneous, emotional response of the heart."[45] Randy Alcorn wrote, "The idea that 'joy is not an emotion' promotes an unbiblical myth."[46]

Now, reading this, you might think, "Well, duh, of course it is." Or, you might think, "Man, I don't agree with that." My encouragement to you is to keep reading. Joy as an emotion is just the starting point. Joy is not *just* an emotion; it's so much more. But we'll get to that.

OUR EMOTIONAL BROKENNESS

If the Scriptures appear to be clear that joy is an emotion, why do so many Christians today believe it's not? It's because emotions are generally misunderstood and, at times, demonized. There can be many factors to this, but I believe a big factor is what culture today promotes about emotions. We live in a very emotionally driven society. We'll hear things like:

> *Do whatever makes you happy.*
> *Follow your heart!*
> *If it feels like the right thing to do, then do it.*

In response to the cultural message, the church has countered the culture with its own messages about emotions. You probably have read books, heard sermons, and heard Natalie in your small group say things like:

> *Don't follow your heart; follow Jesus.*
> *Choose faith over your feelings.*
> *Control your emotions, or your emotions will control you.*

I hear or see some variation of these at least once a week. I've even said them myself. The truth is these messages are not wrong. We shouldn't be led by our emotions because our emotions can lead us astray into sin. We should also follow Jesus even if it doesn't feel good at times. These messages may not be wrong, but the underlying message received is that emotions are *bad*. Emotions are fleeting and unpredictable. Ignore them if you can. Even if you're sad or mad, keep it to yourself. Don't let your emotions get the best of you. Instead, push your emotions down and choose to have a good attitude. "How are you, brother? I'm good, how are you? I'm good." That's the message in our churches, but it's also in our homes, isn't it?

I'm not sure what your home was like growing up, but I guarantee it has affected you. Many of us deal with our emotions the way they were modeled to us. Your mom may have worn her emotions on her sleeves, whereas your dad never showed his emotions. Many of you have never seen your dad cry. Sometimes, the only emotion you saw from your dad was anger.

Your mom may have shown her emotions by being passive aggressive. She wanted to let the whole house know something was wrong without actually saying what was wrong. Her face, demeanor, and her tone said it all.

Then there's "the silence." Days went by with constant avoidance, and no words were said. And if anyone was brave enough to ask, "Are you okay?" the reply was often the infamous "I'm fine." Then, when there was actually a conversation, it ended up being a fight. The volcano of suppressed emotions finally explodes, and the effects are damaging. Can you relate?

As your parents attempted to 'control' their emotions, they also attempted to control yours. Many of us were constantly told, "Be good, don't be bad." Being good meant being on your best behavior. Have a good attitude, not a bad attitude. Be kind and not mean. Be grateful and not entitled. Do as you are told, and don't act out. At any point that we deviate from being "good," we get reprimanded and threatened, especially in public. "Stop crying!" "Stop throwing a fit!" "If you don't stop, I will take you home!" "Cut it out, or I'll take away your toys!" What was your response?

Often, you either shut down or you threw down. You suppress your emotions and put on a face that says, "I'll be good." When you shut down, you probably isolated yourself in some way. You either escape to Watch TV or YouTube, play video games, read books, play outside, play in your room, or scroll social media (depending on how old you are). You went to whatever distracted you from feeling your emotions. Or there came points where you couldn't suppress your emotions anymore, and you chose violence. You may have thrown tantrums by yelling, screaming, kicking, and throwing, all because you just wanted your control back. No matter how you responded, the message you received was that emotions are bad, and you were shamed for showing them. It doesn't matter what you feel, just behave and be good.

That message is what we carry into adulthood, and our responses are the same. We shut down, and we escape to our vices and devices. Whether it's binge-watching a show, drinking, pornography, online shopping, working more, or tomb scrolling our phones, we just want to escape. We're either trying to numb our feelings, or we're trying to feel something because we are numb. And when we can't suppress our feelings any longer, we throw down. We blow up on anyone and everyone. We yell, and we fight. We have become what was modeled to us when we were young. The cycle of broken emotions continues, and if we're not careful, we will repeat the cycle with our kids. Many of us already have.

A quick personal note here. My intention is not to bash anyone or bring shame. The reason our parents struggled with their emotions is that their parents probably did, too. It's a continual cycle passed down from generation to generation. And to be clear, we are 100% responsible for dealing with our emotions. For me, I am a bonafide stuffer. I stuff my emotions down better than anyone, and I've done that my whole life. Then, at my weakest points, I explode in the most unhealthy ways. And now I'm seeing the same thing in my daughter. That's not to say all of her tantrums are justifiable. She threw a fit recently because she wanted to eat Oreos in her bed. Same, but no.

The point is that emotional brokenness is real, and we need to be honest about it. Not only is it affecting us and the ones we love, but it's also affecting our relationship with God.

GOD AND EMOTIONS

This belief of "being good" and "emotions are bad" affects our relationship with God by projecting our broken experiences and emotions onto Him. We may view God as an unemotional being watching over us, ensuring we're "staying in line." Whenever we do step out of line and sin, we think God is mad at us and punishes us for it. In our minds, we feel like God distances Himself from us in disapproval and disgust. We imagine Him saying to us, "Why did you do that again?" or "Why aren't you obeying Me?" or "Stop being bad and just be good." But we can never be good enough. We feel like a screw-up that God is perpetually disappointed in. So then we shut down because of our shame, and we go back to our vices and devices. We feel like we'll never be able to make God happy.

In addition to not being good enough, we believe our emotions are bad, and God is upset that we have them. We imagine Him saying, "Why are you anxious?" or "Why are you sad? or "Why don't you have more faith?" or "Stop being afraid and anxious. You should have joy." We feel like God doesn't care about our emotions; He just wants us to be good. We feel like He's not interested in how we feel but only in how we act.

The truth is God is not like anything that we imagine Him to be. This is where our feelings can deceive us, and what you just read above are examples of that. God is nothing like us or our parents. Where we are emotionally broken, He is emotionally perfect. God is not an unemotionally distant being but an emotionally intimate being. His love and favor aren't dependent on your goodness but on Christ's goodness. That's the beauty of the gospel! When you are in Christ, God is free to love you unconditionally and unlimitedly. His emotions are not fickle or fluctuate like ours; instead, they are fixed. His love and joy are fixed on you, and His anger and wrath are righteously fixed on evil. God doesn't love you because you're good but because you are His.

Let me be clear: emotions are not bad; emotions are good. Emotions are necessary for relationships. A marriage does not last if the husband or wife are not emotionally connected. The ones that are emotionally connected thrive. Emotions are the difference between being a roommate or a spouse. But like anything good that God creates, our emotions are broken because of sin and can be twisted toward evil. Emotions that are meant to bond relationships can also destroy them. Our misuse of emotions has overshadowed the good they were meant for. I believe that has played a significant part in our misunderstanding of joy. I believe God wants to redeem our emotions so that we can connect with Him and others the way we are created to.

God created humans with emotions because He has emotions. That is a way we are image-bearers of Him. In their book *Untangled Emotions*, J. Alasdair Groves and Winston T. Smith wrote, "God gave you emotions to connect you, bind you, and draw you to himself."[47] God cares about how you feel. In fact, Jesus can even empathize with you. Because of Jesus' human nature, He felt how you feel, apart from the effect of sin (Hebrews 4:15). Jesus felt anger (Matthew 21:12-17), anxiety (Luke 22:44), compassion (Matthew 15:32), grief (John 11:35), and *joy* (Luke 10:21). Jesus understands us because He was one of us. He doesn't shame us for our feelings; He wants us to take our feelings to Him.

Jesus modeled this for us in the Garden of Gethsemane right before He was betrayed. When He was overwhelmed with anxiety to the point of sweating blood, He prayed to the Father for help (Luke 22:44). He asked if there was any other way to save us besides dying on the cross. How vulnerable and honest was that? But that's the relationship Jesus had with the Father. He can be honest about how He felt and asked if there was another way. But in the end, Jesus submitted to the Father's will because He trusted Him. You see, God desires our feelings and faith. He wants us to be honest with Him and ask for His help.

David is another example of being emotionally connected with God. He wrote his Psalms in a very raw and honest way. Sometimes, David felt abandoned by God and told God how he felt (Psalm 42). Sometimes, he felt despair because of his situation, wondering if God would deliver him (Psalm 102). There were also Psalms of pure joy for God's love and work in His people's lives (Psalm 98). No matter how David felt, he shared it with God. Think about it: If David was a member of some of our churches, he would be criticized for some of his Psalms. "Oh David, you're being led by your emotions again," or "Oh David, you need to count it all joy." But David's Psalms show us that we can come to God with anything we are feeling and dealing with.

When I was a child, I played outside all the time. Those days, you would knock on someone's door to see if they would come out to play. I'm not sure how much that happens anymore. Anyway, our front yard was the place we always played. We played whiffle ball, capture the flag, basketball, and football all the time. Because we played in our front yard almost every day, we wore out the grass so much that there were just massive dirt and mud spots. It was like the Sandlot! My dad wasn't very happy about that. Since there was so much dirt, I would get absolutely filthy by the time the night ended. Sometimes I was unrecognizable. When it was time to come in for the night, I would come to the screen door, and my mom would say, "No, no, no, go to the hose and wash yourself off before you come in this house!" So, I go to the side of the house, wash myself off, and then come inside to shower and go to bed.

For most of my life, I viewed my relationship with God this way. I have my mess of sin and emotions, and I was not allowed in God's presence with my mess. It was as if Jesus was standing at the door saying, "Go clean yourself up before you come to me." I felt like I needed to get my life together and make myself more presentable to come to Jesus. Have you felt that way? Well, the opposite is true. Jesus isn't turning us away; He's inviting us *in*. He's standing at the door saying, "You can't clean yourself up. Come in, and I will clean you." That's what Jesus desires for you. To come to Him with everything, mess and all. As Jennie Allen wrote, "We think God is waiting for us to pull ourselves together, but actually He is waiting for us to come to Him and fall apart."[48] Jesus desires that for you. He also desires for you to have joy, and He even tells us how we can have it.

HOW TO HAVE JOY

In John 15, Jesus takes everything we have learned about joy and brings it together in one teaching. He even gives us more insight into joy's nature. This passage is part of what's called "The Farewell Discourse" in John's gospel, which is John 14-17. Jesus knew His crucifixion was near, so He shared some final words with His disciples before His impending death. In the middle of His farewell, He used a metaphor that would have been very familiar to his disciples: a vineyard. What was His message? In John 15:1-11 we read:

> "I am the true vine, and my Father is the vinedresser. Every branch in me that does not bear fruit he takes away, and every branch that does bear fruit

he prunes, that it may bear more fruit. Already you are clean because of the word that I have spoken to you. Abide in me, and I in you. As the branch cannot bear fruit by itself, unless it abides in the vine, neither can you, unless you abide in me. I am the vine; you are the branches. Whoever abides in me and I in him, he it is that bears much fruit, for apart from me you can do nothing. If anyone does not abide in me he is thrown away like a branch and withers; and the branches are gathered, thrown into the fire, and burned. If you abide in me, and my words abide in you, ask whatever you wish, and it will be done for you. By this my Father is glorified, that you bear much fruit and so prove to be my disciples. As the Father has loved me, so have I loved you. Abide in my love. If you keep my commandments, you will abide in my love, just as I have kept my Father's commandments and abide in his love. These things I have spoken to you, that my *joy* may be in you, and that your *joy* may be full.

From this teaching, there are four things I would like to highlight:

The Son is the Vine
Jesus says from the very start that He is the *true* vine. Throughout Israel's history, they were often described as God's vine (Psalm 80:9-16, Isaiah 5:1-7, Hosea 10:1-2). But, because of Israel's faithlessness and unfaithfulness, they were producing no fruit.

So Jesus is telling His disciples and us that God has a new *true* vine, and He will produce much fruit.

The vine is the source of life. Without the vine, there are no branches, and there is no fruit. Jesus is saying He is the source of life for His followers and intends to produce fruit through them. But apart from Jesus, we can do nothing. We'll cover more about that in a few moments.

The Father is the Gardener

The Father is the vinedresser, or the "Gardner." He is the overseer of the vineyard. He tends and cares for the vine and the branches with the sole objective of producing fruit. The Gardner tends his vineyard by cutting off dead branches that aren't producing fruit. He also prunes fruit-producing branches so they can produce even more fruit.

This is a picture of what God the Father does with His people. In His sovereignty, The Father oversees the church to ensure it produces spiritual fruit that gives Him glory. The people not producing fruit are evidence of not being connected to Jesus in the first place and are eventually removed. Judas is an example of this. But, those who produce fruit will experience pruning, depicted as trials, suffering, and discipline. Pruning is often painful, but it's purposeful. The Father prunes His branches, producing more spiritual fruit for His glory.

We are the Branches

We are the branches of the vine, and as the branches, we bear the fruit of the vine. This leads to Jesus' main point of His teaching: we can't produce fruit on our own; we must stay connected to Him. We must depend entirely on Jesus to produce real spiritual fruit.

Jesus uses the word "abide" ten times in this passage, which is the Greek word *meno*, sometimes translated as "remain" or "dwell." Here, abiding means staying intimately connected to Jesus. Life will bring ups and downs, sorrow and joy, pain and pleasure, but no matter what, abide in Him. Why? Because Jesus is the source of life, and apart from Him, we can do nothing. Sometimes, we try to be our own vine and produce fruit on our own. But that is not our place. Jesus is the vine, and we are the branches. Our purpose is to abide in Him, and He will produce the fruit.

Joy is a Fruit

Jesus says in verse eleven, "*These things I have spoken to you, that my joy may be in you, and that your joy may be full.*" Jesus' purpose in teaching the vines and branches was to tell us how to have joy! But not just any joy. When we abide in Jesus, His joy is in us. When we are close to Jesus, we can feel His joy in our hearts, and that makes our joy full, like a branch full of grapes so heavy that it has to rest on the ground. He is the vine, we are the branches, and joy is a fruit.

Paul also calls joy a fruit. In Galatians 5:22-23, he lists what is known as the fruit of the Spirit. They are "love, *joy*, peace, patience, kindness, goodness, faithfulness, gentleness, self-control." As we abide in Jesus, the Holy Spirit abides in us and empowers us to follow Jesus so that we can become more and more like Him. In this case, it means having joy just like Jesus does. He wants that for you, and I know you want it, too. That said, we can come to some important conclusions from Jesus' teaching.

Defining Joy

1. ***Jesus produces joy in us; we cannot produce joy on our own.***

    Jesus is the vine, we are the branches, and apart from Him, we can do nothing. Many of us have tried to produce joy on our own, but it is impossible to do with our willpower. We may produce an outward appearance of joy, but it's not real joy.

    When I was a child, we visited my grandparents' house a few times a year. One time, my grandma had a bowl of apples in the center of her dining room table. I was hungry, and those apples sure looked good. I grabbed one of the apples and took a big ole bite out of it. I was shocked when I realized my mouth was full of styrofoam! They were artificial apples from Hobby Lobby for decoration. Boy, was that an unpleasant surprise!

    I think many Christians today have been producing a fake fruit of joy. It looks real on the outside, but on the inside, we know it's not real. We say things like "choose joy," which I always thought meant having a positive attitude or being optimistic and energetic. But that's not what joy is. The problem with "choosing joy" is that we're trying to take control. But joy is not about taking control; it's about surrendering control to Jesus. In light of Jesus' teaching, I would like to reframe "choose joy." The truth is, you can't choose joy; rather, you choose Jesus, and the joy will come.

2. ***Joy is not a superficial emotion; joy is a supernatural one.***

    Part of the hang-up people have about joy being an emotion is the passages that command joy, especially in times of suffering. But in Christ, joy is not a superficial emotion; it's a supernatural one. Joy doesn't come from within ourselves but from abiding in Jesus and being empowered by the Spirit. In times of trouble and suffering, Jesus will command us to do things beyond ourselves. Try "Don't be anxious" or "Do not fear" on for size. Those are commands that are nearly impossible on your own, but Jesus commands those so that you depend on Him.

There was one time Jesus taught a crowd of five thousand (probably triple that with women and children) in a desolate place. The disciples told Jesus that He should send them away into the nearby villages so they could eat and sleep. But Jesus told his disciples, "You give them something to eat" (Mark 6:37). The disciples were so taken back and started freaking out because the task seemed impossible. Jesus asked them to see what food they already had. They came back with five loaves and two fish. Jesus took those and divided them among the people (I will be asking Him how He did this in Heaven someday), and miraculously, everyone ate and was satisfied. They even had twelve baskets left over! Jesus asked his disciples to do something that was beyond themselves so Jesus could show them they just needed to ask Him for help. When we do the natural, Jesus will do the supernatural.

So with commands from the apostles like "Count it all joy, when you face trials of many kinds" (James 1:2-4) and "Rejoice always" (1 Thessalonians 5:16), they are commanding you to do something that is beyond yourself at times. They are not asking you to take control and white knuckle through it. Jesus doesn't just want your obedience; He wants your dependence. Suffering ought to make us more dependent on Him, which then has the opportunity to produce even more joy. Jesus told his disciples,

"Until now you have asked nothing in my name. Ask, and you will receive, that your *joy* may be full" (John 16:24). Rejoicing in suffering is an invitation to go deeper with Him. And when you do, the joy will come.

3. *Joy is rooted in love.*

From the vines and branches passage, as well as the rest of Scripture, we've learned that we can only have abundant joy if we abide in Jesus. Joy is about connection. But the question remains: *How* do we abide? Jesus tells us at the end of the passage: *love.*

Jesus says that He loves us, just as the Father loves Him (John 14:9). Think about that. The same perfect and intimate love the Father has for Jesus, Jesus loves you. Wow! That's hard to believe, isn't it? We feel like there's no way that's true. We feel like we aren't worthy of His love. But to Jesus, you were worth dying for because He loves you. And He has pursued you all your life because He wants you. He doesn't love you because of what you can do for Him; He loves you because you belong to Him.

With that being said, Jesus calls us to abide in His love (John 15:9). Jesus wants us to know of His love, but He also wants us to experience it and live in it. How do we do that? By loving Him back! Jesus says the way we love Him is by keeping His commandments (John 14:15, 15:10). Now, following commands might not seem all that loving, but all of His commands are about love. Jesus says the greatest commands are to love God and others, and all the other commandments in the Bible teach us how to love (Matthew 22:36-40). So naturally, when we follow His commands, we are going to love Him and love others more deeply. But as you may know, following Jesus' commands is difficult. But yet again, abiding is not just about obeying Jesus; it's about depending on Jesus. When we lean into Him to help us love, our relationships will grow deeper. We will delight in Him and have joy knowing Him and loving Him.

This was true for the first-century Christians. Remember what I shared in chapter one? Peter described the Christians in Asia Minor as a people marked by joy. He wrote to them saying, "Though you have not seen him [Jesus], you *love* him. Though you do not now see him, you believe in him and rejoice with joy that is inexpressible and filled with glory" (1 Peter 1:8). The first-century Christians were marked by joy because they were first marked by love. As a church they were abiding in Jesus together. No matter the circumstances, their steadfast love for Jesus and each other produced a steadfast joy that was distinct. I believe Jesus also wants that to be true for twenty-first-century Christians.

Joy Defined

In chapter one, I asked others and yourself to define joy. I believe after research and the revelations we've uncovered from the Scriptures, we can finally define what joy is. I think this will be helpful for all of us as we continue our pursuit of joy. I define joy:

> *Joy is a supernatural emotion empowered by the Holy Spirit when we are deeply connected to Jesus and others.*

In a way, joy is like an abiding meter. If we have a lot of joy, that means we are abiding well. But, if we don't have joy, we likely are not abiding well. So, reflecting on this, why are the twenty-first-century Christians different from the first-century Christians when it comes to joy? As I alluded to in chapter three, our lack of joy is actually revealing a deeper issue. It appears that we don't just have a joy problem; we have a connection problem.

REFLECTION AND DISCUSSION QUESTIONS

1. How did you deal with your emotions growing up? How about today?
2. Do you deal with your emotions today in a way similar to how your parents dealt with them growing up?
3. Do you think your view of emotions has impacted how you interact with God? How so?
4. From the vines and branches passage, what part stood out to you the most?
5. How did you view joy before reading this book? Has your view changed at all? How so?
6. Why do you think love and joy are so closely connected?

CHAPTER FIVE

Joy Idols

Our family has moved seven times in seven years. No, we are not in the circus. Although, that's kind of debatable. It wasn't because of new jobs. In fact, for most of those seven years, we had the same jobs and stayed in the same city. So what gives? Honestly, it wasn't on purpose. Samantha and I lived in a few apartments and then a rental house. Then, we bought our first house and lived there for two years. But we needed something a little bigger for our growing family. We had an opportunity to build a new house just down the road that would suit us, and we took it. Now, here we are!

You would think we enjoy moving by how much we've done it in the last seven years, but I promise we don't. In fact, Samantha told me if we ever have to move again, she's staying, and I'll have to go! Message received.

I think Samantha secretly loves it, though. Moving allows her to flex her organizational skills. She writes detailed descriptions on boxes and uses a color-coded tape system on all the boxes, corresponding to areas where boxes need to go in the new house. She had a paper (aka her master plan) with all the colors and rooms they belonged to.

I was fine with just writing "Kitchen" on the box, but I chose to stay in my lane.

Despite our apparent expertise in moving, we still manage to lose things. After our last move, we could not find Samantha's curling iron. It had us baffled. We looked in all the boxes labeled "master bathroom" with the blue tape but had no luck. As we looked through other boxes while on the hunt, Samantha kept telling me, "I packed that box. I know it's not in there." I thought, "Yeah, but it wasn't in the blue tape boxes either, was it? Do you want curly hair or not?" I trusted my wife, but I just wanted to make sure, so I checked anyway. Lo and behold, she was right; it wasn't in any of those boxes. Come to find out, the elusive curling iron wasn't even in our house! Somehow, it was at my parent's house the whole time. But, at long last, Samantha could have curly hair again, and all was right in the world.

In our pursuit of joy, we've learned that joy comes from being deeply connected to Jesus. We won't find true joy apart from Him. But, out of curiosity, our hearts want to see for ourselves, so we pursue other things anyway. And when we do, we don't find joy. But instead of moving on, we repeatedly go back to these things, hoping to find joy, but we still don't. We're often like me, looking for the curling iron in a box I have already checked a hundred times and hoping it will show up the hundred and first. It's not going to be there. We need to stop looking in those places.

Typically, this is where people will bring up the debate about happiness vs. joy. People will say happiness is a counterfeit joy we pursue instead of real joy. As I shared in chapter four, I don't think that's actually the issue. I believe our issue is much deeper. We aren't pursuing counterfeit joy; we are pursuing counterfeit gods to give us joy. And there lies our connection problem.

PURSUING COUNTERFEIT GODS

Idols have always been a problem for God's people. God commanded, "You shall have no other gods before me" (Exodus 20:3). Even though God commanded His people to have no idols, the local pagan worshiper's lives looked so attractive. They seemed to have prosperous wealth, flourishing crops and fertility, and abundant pleasure. They appeared to have joy. God's people wanted those things, too, so instead of pursuing God for those things, they pursued idols instead. And thousands of years later, we have been lured into the same trap today. We might not have carved statues on our nightstands, but we still pursue idols to give us what we desire.

In his book *Counterfeit Gods,* Tim Keller says an idol "is anything more important to you than God, anything that absorbs your heart and imagination more than God, and anything that you seek to give you what only God can give."[49] That is an excellent framework for evaluating our lives. Here are some good questions to ask yourself:

- Is there anything in my life that I deem more important than God?

- Is there anything that captivates my affection and attention more than God?
- Is there anything I seek to meet my needs and desires instead of God?

As Keller highlighted in his definition, we can make anything an idol. John Calvin once famously said the human heart is a "perpetual forge of idols."[50] In other words, our hearts are idol factories. We constantly pursue worldly things to meet our immediate needs and give us what our hearts desire instead of God. But the idols we pursue never produce the joy we desire. In fact, they make us joyless. These idols are fake vines, producing fruit, but not the kind we want.

When I think of this generation and our idols, I think of King Solomon. He was the wisest and wealthiest ruler of his day and arguably all of history. Solomon had everything we pursue today but in ridiculous abundance. For example, Solomon's net worth was 2 trillion dollars.[51] Yes, trillion with a "T." That is more than Elon Musk, Jeff Bezos, and Bill Gates's net worth combined! In addition to his prosperity, Solomon also had power, fame, possessions, success, and pleasures. You would think all these things would make Solomon the most joyful person on the planet, but in reality, they made him miserable.

It's believed that Solomon wrote the book of Ecclesiastes in his old age as a poetic reflection of his life. As he reflects, he talks about his life "under the sun," which is his way of saying his life apart from God. Solomon shares how He tried to find meaning and joy in life apart from God but couldn't find it. He repeatedly calls things the Hebrew word *hevel*, which means "vanity" or literally "smoke or vapor." As Solomon puts it, pursuing meaning and joy apart from God is like chasing after the wind. What he was looking for was not found under the sun but beyond the sun.

Solomon's appeal to us is not to pursue idols to give us things only God can. Solomon pursued foreign gods and worldly idols to fulfill his heart and give him joy, but they didn't. Solomon tested that experiment in his life and tells us we don't need to repeat the same mistakes. The worldly idols Solomon pursued are the ones we are pursuing today. Solomon highlights these idols, and we're going to unpack them together.

The Idol of Money

What would you do with 2 trillion dollars? Maybe buy an island? Or twenty? Despite Solomon's insane amount of money, he says money will drive you insane. Solomon says, "He who loves money will not be satisfied with money, nor he who loves wealth with his income; this also is vanity" (Ecclesiastes 5:10). Wealth is like chasing after the wind.

Today, we desire to be rich. When I talk to young adults about their goals in life, without fail, they say they want "financial freedom" or to be "financially secure." They want to make six figures or more and live comfortably for the rest of their lives. That's not surprising because that is the Western ideal advertised. Andy Crouch calls this the "system of mammon," which he defines as abundance without dependence.[52] Basically, it's the belief that if you build your life around wealth, you can be free from obligations, dependence, and risk. You can do whatever you want, have whatever you want, and you won't need help from anyone, especially God. We think once we finally reach financial freedom and security, then we'll have joy. All you need to do is serve money, and money will serve you.

But Jesus says you can't serve God and money (Matthew 6:24). He warns His followers about the worship and love of money and how it prevents us from loving and serving Him wholeheartedly. Instead of being dependent on Jesus, we become dependent on money. Instead of building our lives around Him, we build our lives around how much money we make. But what happens when you lose your job, the market crashes, or there's an accident, and you lose everything? Money is a terrible god when you don't have it anymore.

Serving the idol of money promises freedom, but actually, you become a slave to it. You'll always want more, producing the fruit of greed and discontentment. It's like what the billionaire John D. Rockefeller famously said, "How much money does it take to make a man happy? Just one more dollar."[53] The joy you thought money would give you just makes you miserable. But it doesn't have to be that way.

Being wealthy is not the problem. There are plenty of wealthy people who love Jesus and have incredible joy. Why? From the people I know, they are not motivated to build their kingdom. Instead, they are radically motivated to build Jesus' kingdom. They leverage everything they have for ministry. They generously use their house, cars, skills, businesses, and financial resources for the Lord. And they have so much joy doing it! But they didn't start being generous once they became wealthy. They were generous when they had nothing. Generosity is for everyone, and being generous will give you joy. Start today, and you'll fight against the idol of money.

Do you want to be wealthy? How do you spend your money today? Are you motivated by greed or generosity? How we deal with money is crucial because money often funds our worship of other idols.

The Idols of Food and Drink

I love food, and many of us do. My favorite food is Texas brisket. When this Chicago boy first experienced this Texan delicacy, I audibly said, "Where has this been all my life?" Food and drinks are delicious and woven into the fabric of our social lives. These are good things, but even food and drinks can become idols if we aren't careful. These idols are the least talked about in churches but are some of the most prominent. Solomon, reflecting on experimenting with self-indulgence, wrote, "I said in my heart, "Come now, I will test you with pleasure; enjoy yourself…I searched with my heart how to cheer my body with wine…" and that too was vanity (Ecclesiastes 2:1, 3a).

We make food and drinks our idol for comfort. When stressed or sad, we often turn to food and drinks to feel better. We just want some temporary relief. So, we turn to things that we enjoy. We eat out, buy craft coffee, and go to the gas station for snacks or a 32oz cheap soda. It's as if this voice says, "Hey, this will make you feel better," or "Hey, you had a tough day; you deserve to treat yourself." Places are even advertising that their product will give you joy. Today, if you get a Starbucks drink, the cup says, "Let us add a little joy to your day." But, a true principle here, as well as other idols we'll get into, is this: just because you enjoy it doesn't mean it will give you joy.

Food and drinks often act as an escape from reality. This is especially true when we overeat or drink to the point of intoxication. We may temporarily feel better when we indulge, but it's only an illusion. Reality will set back in; we will need comfort again, and we will repeat the cycle. This becomes a ruthless and unhealthy habit in our lives. We become dependent and addicted to caffeine, sugar, and alcohol, producing the fruit of gluttony and drunkenness.

We aren't supposed to pursue food and drinks to comfort us. Instead, we are supposed to pursue the God of all comfort (2 Corinthians 1:3). Jesus is the only one who will bring peace to your heart. It's okay to enjoy your favorite food or drink; just be careful not to become dependent on them or indulge in unhealthy ways. Ultimately, the best way to enjoy food and drinks is when we enjoy them with Jesus and others. Whether it's family, friends, co-workers, neighbors, or strangers, the table brings us together, giving us great joy. Yes, it brings nourishment to your body, but also nourishment to your soul.

Do you pursue food or drinks for comfort? Do you find yourself in a habit of overeating or drinking? Are you dependent on certain foods or drinks?

The Idol of Possessions

We really love our stuff. We live in a consumerist and materialistic society, where we spend our money not just for our needs but out of desire. Solomon lived this way, too. He acquired gold and silver, palaces, luxurious clothes, chariots, land, and thrones.

But his proudest possession was his livestock. He said, "I had also great possessions of herds and flocks, more than any who had been before me in Jerusalem" (Ecclesiastes 2:7cd). Today, people flex their wealth by their number of cars, but Solomon's flex was his number of cows!

Possessions are our idols for status and satisfaction. We judge each other by the brands we wear, the cars we drive, and the size of our homes. When we buy things, we aren't just buying a product but an image. We want people to think a certain way about us based on the things we have. So, we often overspend on products we don't need to maintain this image.

We also think that buying things will satisfy us. We see something advertised on social media, go on Amazon, and impulse buy. Then, it shows up at our door the next day. We also see what others have, and we want it too. So, we buy new shoes, the newest phone, or the newest popular water cup (not trying to call you out, but you know who you are) to be like everyone else. We are shown advertisements that these things will satisfy us and even give us joy! The other day, I saw a Hyundai commercial with their latest promotion saying, "There's joy in every journey." So, if I buy a Hyundai, will I have joy every time I drive it? Where do I sign? Can I get it in red?

Our problem is not just about wanting new things. We are attached to old things as well. Did you know the last 20 years have been called the "Storage Unit Boom." From 2000-2019, storage units grew 50% in the US, with 50,000 storage units currently. That growth rate beat the growth of McDonalds in the same amount of time.[54] Why? We love our stuff! We have run out of room in our houses and will pay a monthly fee to keep all of it in a giant metal box. What does this say about us?

Jesus warned us about making possessions an idol. In his gospel, Luke compares two rich men with many possessions. Jesus told one young rich man to give away his possessions and follow Him, but he couldn't because he loved his stuff too much (Luke 18:18-30). Then Jesus met a rich tax collector named Zacchaeus, who repented and gave away everything to follow Jesus (Luke 19:1-10). Am I saying you need to get rid of all your stuff? No. But, if Jesus asked you to get rid of your stuff, is there anything you would not be willing to let go of? We all need to do an honest inventory of our stuff and why we have it. Jesus tells us life is not about status or stuff; it's about serving and loving Him.

Is there a status you're trying to keep with your stuff? How often do you buy something just because you want it? Is there anything you are not willing to get rid of? Why?

The Idol of Entertainment

We live in environments of constant entertainment. We have TVs in almost every room in our homes. We have all the different streaming services that end with a "plus." We have the latest and greatest gaming systems. We have our favorite sports teams that we obsessively follow and watch. We have smartphones, which are entertainment in our pockets whenever we need them. For Solomon, entertainment definitely looked different, but he still pursued it. He wrote, "I said of laughter, 'It is mad,' and of pleasure, 'What use is it?' and later, "I got singers, both men and women" (Ecclesiastes 2:2,8bc). You may have Spotify, but do you have your own personal singers?

The idol of entertainment today takes our time and attention away from God. Today, the average young adult is on pace to spend one-third of their life scrolling social media, binge-watching shows, and playing video games.[55] For perspective, the other thirds are spent sleeping and working. We may not be worshiping carved images, but we are worshiping images, aren't we? But it's not just because we enjoy funny YouTube videos or Netflix dramas. Our screens are another way we cope with life, specifically with our thoughts and feelings.

Tyler Staton said in a podcast, "When the mind is idle, it goes to negative places."[56] Think about it: What do you think about when you are driving, sitting on the couch, standing in line, or lying in bed? Often, we think about bad things we've done, things we didn't get done at work, replaying negative situations or conversations, or being anxious about the days to come. So what do we do? We turn on the music or turn to our screens to distract us from our boredom, shame, anxiety, and worry. Instead of focusing our attention on God and bringing our thoughts and feelings to Him, we give our attention to our idol to make us feel better. And in an effort to escape our thoughts and feelings, the idol of entertainment produces more anxiety and depression. So why do we keep coming back to it?

Dr. Cal Newport said social media is designed like a slot machine. Social media companies hired "Attention Engineers" who design Las Vegas Casinos to help make these platforms as addictive as possible.[57] Why? Well, just like casinos, those companies make money the more time you spend on them. They monetize your attention. You get a hit of dopamine (feel-good neurotransmitter), and they get your data and sell it. And we always come back for more because we enjoy being entertained. But again, just because you enjoy it doesn't mean it will give you joy. And your pocket slot machine won't.

Here's the truth: our scrolling and binging is shaping us. The issue isn't just about stealing our attention but also about what we give our attention to. Jesus said the eyes are the lamp of the body, and whatever we give our attention to will fill us with either light or darkness (Matthew 6:22-23). Often, the content we consume is overly sexual, vulgar, and violent. Unfortunately, we've become so desensitized by darkness that we no longer blush at evil but instead are entertained by it. Candidly, we are not abiding in Jesus when we are; we are abiding in darkness. That is hurting your relationship with Him. This is something we have to wrestle with, and we will explore this more in the next chapter.

What do you do when your mind is idle? How many hours a day do you spend in front of a screen (not including work)? What entertains you?

The Idols of Sex and Relationships

Yup, we're going there. But don't worry, this isn't going to be the weird sex talk you had as a preteen. Hopefully.

Whether you're single, dating, engaged, or married, all of us desire intimacy, love, and connection. The reason is that you were designed for them. God created us to pursue intimacy with Him, but also to pursue it with our spouse. When God created Adam, He said it was not good for him (humanity) to be alone, so God created Eve (Genesis 2:18). They were created to have intimacy with God and each other. But because sin has entered the picture, our desires are broken, and we pursue intimacy outside of God's design.

That's what Solomon did. Solomon disregarded God's command and pursued women outside of Israel. Solomon's heart turned away from God because he pursued these women (1 Kings 11:9). He also disregarded God's design for marriage by having 700 wives and 300 concubines (1 Kings 11:3, Ecclesiastes 2:8d). Yeah. Pretty awful, right? That sounds like a reality TV show. But, as extreme and horrendous as Solomon's choices were, we also disregard God's command and design for relationships and sex. We desire intimacy, but we choose to pursue it our way, and by doing so, we make people and sex our idols.

We believe a person will fulfill us and give us joy. We see rom-coms, Hallmark movies, and dating reality shows advertising romance and intimacy, and we want that, too. So today, you may be dating for fun. You're dating people because of their superficial qualities (attractiveness) instead of spiritual fruit (fruit of the Spirit). The people you date are just objects of amusement. But once the flame fades and the fun stops, so does the relationship.

Others of us are dependent on our relationships. You may only stay single for a short time because relationships are where you pursue attention, value, and affection. You become dependent on this person, and when you break up, it's devastating. To fill the void and to feel better, you get back on the dating apps and are quick to swipe right.

And many of us are pursuing a spouse. Like the shows and movies, you want to find "the one" who will be perfect for you. You think that person will finally complete you. In your pursuit of the one, you'll struggle to commit because of differences in opinions or minor personality flaws. Then you'll move on to the next relationship and then the next in search of your perfect person. This is what some call FOBO, which stands for Fear of Better Options.[58] Your eyes are always wandering, searching for someone prettier, funnier, smarter, and better. Because of this, you may struggle to commit because of the fear of a better option. Or you may commit prematurely because of the fear of being alone. Instead of keeping a high standard, you compromise when you shouldn't have. An area that we are very willing to compromise on is sex.

God created sex for marriage for a husband and wife to enjoy, as well as procreate. Sex is one of the strongest and most natural ways we feel pleasure. That's why people pursue sex outside of God's design to have it. Our culture idolizes and worships sex. The shows we watch contain Hollywood romances of casual sex and adultery. Our culture promotes sexual freedom to be expressed however they would like. Have sex with whoever you want, whenever you want. People even find their identity in their sexuality. And, of course, there is the existence of pornography. All these things advertise pleasure and intimacy, but this is a false advertisement.

Specifically, pornography is a major issue. Did you know that the porn industry generates more revenue than ABC, NBC, and CBS revenues combined, and more than the NFL, NBA, and MLB revenues combined? Also, more people view internet pornography every month than Amazon, X (formerly Twitter), and Netflix combined.[59] Let that sit in for a second. How could this be? It's because pornography promotes pleasure without connection. It's an escape from reality that offers sexual release without relationship or risk. And that's a serious problem. Sex was designed to bond a husband and wife physically, spiritually, and emotionally. So when you read, look, or watch pornography, you try to bond with your book or device, but you can't. This leaves an empty void within you. So what do you do? You keep going back to it, continuing the relentless cycle of pleasure, pain, and shame. Also, porn is another example where we are entertained by darkness, and it's extremely costly. It leads to sexual dysfunction, addiction, abuse, affairs, and even divorce. Sin will never give you joy. It only destroys your life.

Let me be clear, not one person is going to fulfill you; only Jesus can. You're not half a person who needs someone else to make you complete. You are complete in Christ. Your spouse isn't meant to complete you but compliments you. Pursue intimacy with Jesus before pursuing intimacy with anyone else. Don't pursue sex outside of marriage. You think you can have intimacy and joy outside God's design, but you can't. Sex in marriage is blessed, and there is great joy in God's loving boundaries. If you're struggling with porn, talk to someone. You aren't meant to suffer silently. Freedom and redemption are possible through Jesus and others!

Does your relationship bring you closer to Jesus or away from Him? Do you look at, watch, listen to, or read pornography? Have you told anyone about it yet? Will you?

The Idol of Achievements

Are you a high achiever? This is to all the valedictorians, summa cum laude's, all-conference, goal-oriented, Enneagram 3, ubersuccessful individuals. You are the one who sets a goal, and you will do whatever it takes to accomplish it. Solomon was a high achiever, too. He was always busy overseeing construction projects for homes, vineyards, gardens, parks, and pools. His greatest accomplishment was constructing the temple in Jerusalem, which was magnificent in every way. But reflecting on all he had accomplished, Solomon said in Ecclesiastes 2:11, "When I considered all that I had accomplished and what I had labored to achieve, I found everything to be futile and a pursuit of the wind" (CSB). So, is Solomon saying achieving is worthless? No, but your motivation might be an idol.

Many of us are driven to achieve because we seek the attention and approval of others who then become idols in our lives. We want to be seen and noticed for the things we do, sometimes even by the people who are closest to us. Deep down, we are attempting to prove our worth. Sometimes, we want to prove people right or prove people wrong. So this drives us to run the marathon, get the degree, write the book, or get the promotion. We want to feel significant, so we feel like we have to do something significant.

If achievement is your idol, failure is often devastating. If you receive criticism or correction, you often get defensive. The reason is that you think your worth is dependent on your performance. If you don't perform well, you feel worthless and want to avoid that. So, you are driven to succeed again to regain and maintain your worth.

Then, when we succeed, people praise us, which we like—a lot. And we want more of it. So we keep chasing the accolades and achieve more and more. We think if we achieve everything we want, then joy will be our prize. But like Solomon and other high achievers, in the end, you'll achieve everything you've ever wanted, hit the wall, and think, "Is this really it?" Instead of being full of joy, you're full of despair.

The truth is you don't have to achieve significant things to earn approval or be seen. Jesus sees you. Jesus approves of you. You don't have to perform to be accepted by Him. He is so proud of you, whether you achieve great things or not. This is not to say working hard or achieving doesn't matter. But, it comes back to your motivation. You should work hard for His glory, not for your own. That will give you joy.

What's motivating you to achieve? Are you seeking attention and approval from others? Are you doing things to receive the praise of people or God?

The Idol of Career

When you were a child, what did you want to be when you grew up? For me, I wanted to be a baseball player. Unfortunately, having a weak arm and being slow and short was not the right combination to be the next Derek Jeter. So, I had to come up with a backup plan. I remember when I was a teenager, I prayed, "Lord, I'll do anything; just don't make me a pastor." Oh, the irony.

Did you end up being what you wanted? We rarely do. Many of us pick careers because of the money. Or we worked a job when we were younger and worked our way up the company ladder. Or we follow in our parent's footsteps. That's what happened with Solomon. His dad was king, and Solomon took over the kingdom. He was the boss.

Work is a part of God's design, but even our work can be an idol. Often, we look to our jobs to find our identity and purpose.

We think what we do for work is who we are. When someone asks us what we do for work, our common response is, "I am a _____." For some, you take great pride in your career. You love telling people who you are and what you do for work. For others, you don't like your job or feel lost and unsure of what you're supposed to do and who you're supposed to be. Either way, if your identity is in your work, it's often devastating when you don't have a job or lose your job because it's like you've also lost your identity. The same is true for those who retire or need to change careers. *What do I do now? Who am I?*

Work is often where we find our purpose as well. Many of us think our purpose has to do with our personalities, skills, and passions. We think our jobs are where we exercise these qualities that are unique to us. Others find their purpose in what work provides them. For example, many believe their purpose is to make a lot of money and provide for their family. Others think their purpose is to be the boss, so they work to climb the career ladder or choose to be self-employed. No matter what you think your purpose is, your purpose will drive your priorities. For example, if you believe your purpose is to make a lot of money or get a promotion, you will prioritize work over other things to make the sale, get the raise, and earn the title. But at what cost?

If you serve the idol of career, work often takes priority over more important things like family, relationships, and church. For some, work actually becomes an escape from those things. The common excuse is, "Sorry, I have to work." So you miss games, parties, dinners, small groups, Saturday afternoons, and Sunday service. You're so busy pursuing the money, the title, and the stuff that you become alone and burnt out. Your family resents you, you're a stranger at your church, and you're disconnected from God. You may be working to put food on the table, but your family just wants you at the table. Being a workaholic will never give you joy but prevent you from having it.

Your identity is not in your job; it's in Jesus. It's not about what you do; it's about who you belong to. You belong to God and are His beloved child (John 1:12). Your titles may change in your lifetime, but your identity will never change. The same goes for your purpose. Your purpose isn't your job, but your purpose is to glorify God everywhere, including your job. Whether you're a barista, a real estate agent, a plumber, or a CEO, your purpose will remain the same. But your faith and your family will always take priority. Ultimately, Jesus is our boss, and our job is to work hard and win hearts for Him. And when you do, your job will give you joy.

The Idol of Fame

Above, I asked what you wanted to be when you grew up. If you were to ask young people today that question, what do you think the number one answer would be? Naturally, you would think of the classics like athletes, doctors, teachers, nurses, or construction workers. However, the number one job young people want today is to be an *influencer*.[60] They want to work on social media platforms like TikTok or YouTube to create content people follow and make money doing it. Solomon was a kind of influencer in his day. People traveled from all over the world to hear Solomon's wisdom. He created content by writing 3000 proverbs and 1005 songs (1 Kings 4:32), some of which we still read and sing today. But, for him, all of that, too, was vanity.

Today, we have an idol of fame. Not only do we idolize famous people like our favorite athletes, artists, and social media influencers, but some of us desire to be famous ourselves. We desire to be known and loved by others. We fantasize about being noticed in public and being asked for selfies and autographs. At the core, we desire to be worshiped, and that is very dangerous.

Please hear me: influence and fame are not inherently bad things. Influence can be a God-given for His will. There are also famous people who love Jesus and use their platform to glorify Him. But influence and fame become dangerous when we desire it to glorify ourselves. Building a platform for your selfish gain is not good and will lead you astray. We've seen it too many times before. We've also been guilty of giving platforms to talented people whose character wasn't ready for it, and they have fallen. Hard. We've seen this in the world, but especially in the church. We must be careful and prayerful about how we deal with influence and fame today. We have to check our motives constantly.

There is a difference between being noticed and being known. People may notice you in public, but they don't know you. Our desire is to be deeply known by others. Jesus sees you, knows you, and loves you. You don't need to pursue fame to feel significant. You are significant to Him. You don't need a platform to bring Him glory. Bring Him glory in your everyday life. And if He does give you influence, use it for Him, not for yourself.

Do you desire to be famous? Are you using your platform to glorify Jesus or yourself? What are you pursuing to meet your desire to be deeply known?

CONCLUSION

These are the idols we pursue instead of pursuing Jesus. I have struggled with many of these, and I'm sure you have too. What I've learned about these idols is they all have one thing in common. They offer some kind of control. When we feel like there is a lack of control in our lives, we try to grab control instead of trusting that God is in control. In an effort to gain control, we turn to idols to meet our needs and desires. And when we think we've actually gained control, we actually lose control of our lives.

These idols promise great things for what seems like a very small price. If you give your money, love, time, effort, affection, attention, and focus, you will get what you desire. At first, it may feel like it worked. So, we keep coming back for more. But over time, our idols will demand more and deliver less. So then we overwork, overeat, overdrink, and binge to pursue what we once experienced. But our idols will ask for more and more while giving less and less until they eventually demand everything and give nothing.

In college, I read a story about a skylark and worms. There was once a skylark who flew over the desert in search of food. It was a tough time for all living creatures, but especially birds. The skylark became tired, hungry, and restless in his search.

But one day, while flying overhead, the skylark spotted a peddler selling worms! The peddler shouted, "Come right up! Two worms for one feather!" The skylark thought, "I have hundreds of feathers; I can spare one and get two worms! Such a small sacrifice for such a big reward." The skylark excitedly handed over one feather for two delicious, juicy worms.

The next day, the skylark swooped down and paid the peddler a visit again—one feather for two worms. The skylark gladly partook, and his belly was full! This went on for several days. One day, after eating his worms, the skylark attempted to fly. Instead of soaring as he usually does, he plummeted to the ground. He realized his feathers were so bare that he could no longer fly. "What am I going to do?" The skylark thought of an idea. He went into the wilderness to try to find some worms. After several days in the heat and a basket of worms, he revisited the peddler.

"Here are enough worms to exchange for my feathers. I would like them back, please." The devil, disguised as the peddler, laughed and replied, "You can't have your feathers back! You got your worms, and I have your feathers. After all, a deal is a deal." The peddler then disappeared, and the skylark was left broken and unable to fly.

Jesus' heart breaks when we give away our feathers for worms. But His heart breaks even more when we try to buy our feathers back, for only He can restore our feathers.[61] Many of us have been pursuing idols to give us joy, but honestly, only Jesus can provide it. Without knowing it, our idols have been taking from us the things most precious to us, leaving us empty, broken, and joyless.

We need to stop pursuing our idols and pursue Jesus, who will restore our feathers and help us fly again. Are you ready to have the joy you were created for? Next, we will learn how to abide in Jesus so that we can have the joy we all truly desire.

REFLECTION AND DISCUSSION QUESTIONS

1. Of the eight idols shared in the chapter, what are the top three you see in the world today?
2. Of the eight idols shared in the chapter, which one do you struggle with the most?
3. Of the eight idols, which one will be the hardest for you to stop pursuing?
4. In what ways do you need to pursue Jesus instead of pursuing your idol?
5. What steps will you take to prevent you from pursuing these idols?
6. What steps will you take to help you pursue Jesus every day?

CHAPTER SIX
Abiding Joy

"Jared, you're going to have to make some serious changes," said the doctor.

Two years ago, I was having severe health issues. To spare you the details, my throat was abnormally swollen all the time, and I was having trouble eating. I always felt sick, so I regularly ate crackers at mealtimes. Cheez-Its for dinner is not exactly the healthiest lifestyle. So, Samantha convinced me to go to the doctor.

What I learned about myself changed my life. I was diagnosed with a rare auto-immune disorder, in which I had to eliminate all dairy and gluten from my diet. When the doctor told me that news, I blacked out. I was in complete shock. I lived my whole life eating dairy and gluten with no problems at all. I'm the guy who would eat a bowl of ice cream every night before bed. I would eat whole pizzas by myself. But, no more ice cream, pizza, cheeseburgers, queso, pasta, or anything delicious.

Everything I loved to eat, I couldn't have anymore. What I was eating was making me sick.

I drastically changed my diet that summer, cutting out all dairy and gluten. As difficult as that was, I started feeling much better within a few weeks. But, as time passed, I had trouble accepting my new normal. So here and there, I would compromise a little and eat a cookie, Cheetos, or queso. But when I did, I started feeling sick again, and I hated feeling sick. Deep down, I knew I needed to make the necessary sacrifices because I was only hurting myself.

Since that summer, I have been entirely dairy-free and gluten-free, and I feel great! I've learned a couple things on this journey. First, I realized that it's not just about cutting food out but replacing it with food you can have and enjoy. For example, instead of ordering queso, I order guacamole (so good). Secondly, I learned that when you change your diet, your appetite will also change. I no longer crave cheese, bread, or ice cream because I know they'll make me sick. Instead, I crave taco bowls and popcorn—all the time! Overall, the changes were initially difficult, but I feel like I have my life back, and my joy has been restored.

Similarly, the idols we're pursuing have made our hearts sick. Like me, many of us are unaware that we've been pursuing idols to give us joy. Hopefully, chapter five was helpful to you and brought some clarity to your struggle. For others, you may be aware of the idols you've been pursuing, but you are struggling to let go and accept the sacrifices you need to make. Maybe you've tried in the past, but small compromises have led to big compromises, and you find yourself back into old habits and practices that make you feel sick and joyless. Trust me, I understand, not just from a food standpoint but also from following Jesus. So, why do we struggle so much?

Paul explains there is a battle waging in us between our flesh and the Holy Spirit. Your flesh is your broken, sinful nature that is bent toward instant gratification and selfish ambition. The flesh wants to pursue worldly things to meet your desires, even outside God's commands and design. When you were an unbeliever, your flesh was the master, always calling the shots and driving your decisions and actions. But, when you became a follower of Jesus, He placed the Holy Spirit in you, and now there is competition for the driver's seat of your life. Instead of pursuing worldly idols, the Spirit desires you to pursue Jesus with your whole heart. Right now, the flesh and Holy Spirit are fighting for control in you. Who wins? The one that you *feed*.

For clarity, this is not dualism. Your flesh and the Holy Spirit are not equals like the devil is on one shoulder and an angel on the other whispering in your ear what to do. The reality is that your flesh is your old self, and the Spirit is helping you become your new self. Your old self is trying to stay alive and be in control. But, the Spirit is supernaturally helping you become your new self. He is slowly killing off your old self and empowering you to live your new self in Christ. The theological word for this is "sanctification" – the process of Christ changing us to be holy and like Him through the power of the Holy Spirit. Although this is a work of the Spirit in us, we also have a part in this battle.

It is our responsibility to feed the Holy Spirit and starve our flesh. Not with food (although that may apply), but with our time, what we watch, what we give our attention to, how we spend our money, what we think about, what we say, and what we do. Everything we do is either feeding our flesh or feeding the Spirit. When we feed the flesh, we are feeding our old self and its desires, which disconnects us from Jesus. But when we feed the Spirit, we feed our new self, growing in a deeper connection with Jesus. It is our responsibility to starve the flesh and feed the Spirit, but we can't do it alone. We need to abide, which leads us back to the vines and branches.

I love Jerry Bridges' summary of John 15, saying abiding is all about "personal responsibility and total dependence."[62] We are responsible for abiding in Jesus, but He knows we can't do it in our willpower. That's why Jesus gave us the Holy Spirit to abide in us and empower us to abide in Him. Paul says in Galatians 5:16, "Walk by the Spirit, and you will not gratify the desires of the flesh." Remember, if you do the natural, He will do the supernatural in and through you. As Paul says, abiding is not a sprint; it's a walk. Every day, you have an opportunity to take a step with the Spirit, bringing you closer to your Savior. And the more we starve the flesh and feed the Spirit, the more He will change our spiritual appetite and desires. You will find yourself craving Jesus more and more and be disinterested in the fleshly idols you once pursued. You will be inwardly renewed day by day (1 Corinthians 4:16).

Remember, joy is a supernatural emotion empowered by the Holy Spirit when we are deeply connected to Jesus and others. In this chapter, we will explore the ways we can grow our deep connection with Jesus or, in His words, how to abide in Him. So, where do we begin? We'll start where everything starts: your *mind*.

ABIDE IN YOUR MIND

A question to consider is: *What do you dwell on?* In other words, what do you think about the most? This is so important because what you dwell on manifests itself in your life. When you dwell on the past, it makes you sad, shameful, and bitter. When you dwell on the future, it makes you anxious and worried. When you dwell on what you don't have, you become discontent and jealous of others. When you dwell on how people hurt you, it makes you angry and resentful. When you dwell on your failures, it makes you discouraged and afraid. When you dwell on your suffering, you feel hopeless and despair. But when you dwell on Jesus, you are full of joy! So, how do we dwell on Jesus and not on other things? Here are a few ways to help.

Reject and Replace

You can't control the thoughts that come into your mind, but you can choose to dwell on them or not. As we covered in the last chapter, when our mind is idle, it often goes to negative places. Instead of dealing with our negative thoughts well, we either distract ourselves from them or dwell on them. But, instead of distracting or dwelling, we need to reject and replace.

First, we have to examine our thoughts. Paul says to take every thought captive and make it obedient to Christ (2 Corinthians 10:5). The picture is like arresting a suspect and bringing them in for questioning. For us, we need to arrest our thoughts and bring them to Jesus for interrogation and examination against God's Word. Some questions to ask yourself are: Why did I have this thought? Is this thought true? Is this thought helpful or harmful to me or others? If I dwell on this thought, could it lead to sin? All these questions can be helpful, but one question that can act as a screen for all your thoughts is this: *Does this thought help me abide in Jesus?* If the answer is yes, pursue it. But if not, reject it. Ask Jesus to remove the thought from your mind and help you not to dwell on it.

A quick note of clarification. There is a difference between being tempted (when a thought comes to mind) and actually sinning (when we dwell and indulge in it). For example, you may see someone at the grocery store and think they are attractive. That is not a sin. But, if your eyes linger and your mind dwells on them, and your thoughts become sexual, then you have lusted and sinned. And Jesus says, if you just look at someone lustfully, you've committed adultery in your heart (Matthew 5:28). Yes, the eyes are involved, which we will get to, but the sin happened in your mind. In addition to lust, this can be true for anger, judging, pride, envy, and hate. We sin when we dwell on these things. So, we must cut sin off at the root of our minds before it produces evil fruit in our hearts and lives.

After examining our thoughts against God's Word, we replace them with God's Word. Jesus was the perfect example of this in Matthew 4:1-11. Jesus fasted in the desert wilderness for 40 days, feeling tired, hungry, and weak. While Jesus was vulnerable, Satan came and tempted Jesus three times. After each time Jesus was tempted, He rejected Satan's offer and responded with, "For it is written." Jesus quoted several passages from Deuteronomy to reject Satan's temptations and replace them with truth. Now, Jesus didn't have a copy of the Scriptures in the desert with Him; those words were written on His heart. He was ready to examine, reject, and replace any thought or temptation that came His way. If we are to abide in Jesus, we ought to do the same. How do we do it? Let's explore that next.

Memorize and Meditate

How many Bible verses do you have memorized? I don't ask that to make you feel bad if you don't have many or any. Instead, I want you to feel excited about something new you haven't exercised in a while or explored before.

Memorizing Scripture is truly a lost discipline today. Of course, there are children's programs like Awana's that teach and train kids to memorize Scripture, but beyond that, memorization is lost, especially with adults. The biggest battle is getting people to read their Bible, let alone memorize it! But back in biblical times, people had to rely on their memory. They didn't have five copies of the Scriptures and an app on their phone. Often they would memorize whole passages of Scriptures from the Psalms and Prophets. Even young Jewish boys memorized the Torah, which is the first five books of the Bible. That's 5845 verses! Now, they didn't do this just to know the Bible. They did it to store it in their minds and hearts to defend against sin and dwell on truth. As Psalm 119:11 says, "I have stored up your word in my heart, that I might not sin against you." As we abide in Jesus, we should do the same. As you memorize Scripture, you will not only know it but also live it. The Spirit will change you from the inside out.

Here's a challenge for you: Memorize one verse every week. Just one verse. That seems pretty doable, right? To make it fun, invite others to do it with you! If you were to take me up on my challenge, you would memorize 52 verses in one year. If you were to keep going, you'd memorize 104 verses in two years. Just for perspective, that is exactly the number of verses in Philippians! Yes, you could memorize a whole book of the Bible. I know that's a crazy big picture, but I want you to see what's possible. Consistently doing something small for a long time can lead to big results, in this case, an abiding mind full of Jesus and His Word. No matter how you go about it, just start small and don't stop. This is just a starting point. Believe me, you are capable of memorizing way more than you think you can. If you want to learn more about how to memorize Scripture, check out the Bible Memory Goal YouTube channel.

Memorizing Scripture can also help you meditate on Scripture. Now, Christians can get uncomfortable with meditation, thinking it's a practice for other religions such as Hinduism or Buddhism. But meditation has been a practice of God's people for thousands of years. Meditation is simply to focus deeply on something for an extended time, in this case, Scripture! Psalm 119:97 says, "Oh, how I love your law! It is my meditation all the day." Psalm 104:34 says, "May my meditation be pleasing to him, for I *rejoice* in the Lord." Meditating on God's Word can give us great joy! So, how do we meditate? Here's a simple guide:

1. Find Your Place
2. Grab Your Bible
3. Take Your Time

There is no perfect time to meditate. You might be a morning person, so you can do it then. Or you might be a night person and like to do it before bed. The place is not important either. It can be in your bedroom, back patio, kitchen table, couch, desk at work, or car. No matter the time and place, the goal is to find a place and create space between you and distractions. Meditation time is not a Bible study, although you can incorporate it into your daily Bible study or "quiet time." All you do is pick out a small part of your Bible reading and take time to meditate on it.

The picture of meditation is like a cow chewing cud. I know it's not the prettiest image, but it's what we ought to do with God's Word in our minds. We don't just consume it; we chew on it. We ponder it. We let it sink deep into our minds and hearts. Read it fast. Read it slowly. Read it emphasizing different words. Focus all your attention on those verses.

Meditation only takes a few minutes, but you can continue to meditate on what you read throughout the day or as you fall asleep. A study showed that people who meditate on Scripture experienced less stress, less depression, and sleep better.[63] Why? It's because when you choose to dwell on Scripture instead of negative thoughts, it changes you. So, instead of stressing, meditate on Scripture. Instead of scrolling yourself to sleep, meditate on Scripture. If you want additional help in meditation, you can download the app "Abide," which will coach you.

Remember and Reflect

Are you a forgetful person? Many of us are. We forget about appointments, birthdays, anniversaries, or where we put our keys. To help us out, we have calendars, Facebook (it's the only way I know people's birthdays), reminders on our phones, and we write things down. Samantha is so grateful for the "Ping my iPhone" feature because she constantly forgets where she put her phone. Can you relate?

Just like we are forgetful daily, the one we forget most is God. But it's not just our problem. Forgetfulness has always been a problem with God's people. So, knowing that humans are forgetful, God often instructed His people to build altars, write events down, institute festivals, and write songs to remember God and what He's done for them. Why? Because when we remember God's faithfulness in the past, it gives us confidence in the present and hope for the future. And as I shared in chapter two, reflecting on the past was a major theme for people's joy. So, here are a few ways that can help you remember and reflect:

Physical Reminders: Physical reminders symbolize meaningful times or events from our journey with Jesus. Whatever it is, make it visible where you'll see it every day. For example, I have a prosthetic leg in my office. No, I didn't steal someone's leg. Prosthetics was my original career path, and I have it from school. It reminds me daily that I can make plans for my life, but ultimately, God is in control and has a plan for me. Also, it's a great conversation starter!

Journaling: Write about the times of blessings, joy, sorrows, and heartaches. The goal is to be consistent. Then, you'll see God's hand as He works through your life. Also, write to your future self. Go back and read old journals. Sometimes, your past self can encourage your present self. God can use anything, even your own words.

Pictures: Why do you take pictures or post on social media? Probably because you want to look back and reflect on moments from the past! So, go through your photos on your phone and create an album highlighting big life moments and spiritual markers. You can regularly look at those pictures to remember

God's faithfulness. Instead of looking at other people's pictures that make you depressed (social media), look at your pictures that give you hope and joy.

Music: Music is like a time machine for our minds. When we hear a song on the radio or Spotify, it takes us back to a certain time in our lives and even to specific memories. Music fills our minds with words and stirs our emotions. I encourage you to create a playlist of meaningful songs to you and your life and remind you of Jesus. Listen to it often!

Pause and Ponder

"Daddy, what is heaven like?" Ellie asked me that question in the car one night after church. After being lost for words, I told her it's where God lives, an incredible place of perfect love, peace, and joy, and someday we'll be there with Him. I thought that was a good answer! After this talk with Ellie, I realized I hadn't thought deeply about heaven or God in a long time. We talk about heaven, but do we *think* about heaven? We talk about God, but do we *think* about God? We talk about the promises of God, but do we *think* about the promises of God? When was the last time you just sat, walked, or laid down and pondered God and heaven?

This is actually a concern for this generation. Since we are constantly bombarded with distractions, entertainment, and everyday life, we struggle to think deeply about the things of God. Because of this, Ben Stuart said the concern for this generation is that our minds constantly dwell in shallow places, hindering our growth. Like a fish trying to grow up in a rain puddle, we can't be who we were created to be if we stay in shallow places. Rather, our minds need to dwell in deeper places for growth and flourishing. The danger of staying shallow rather than exploring the deep is that this generation will stand in awe of nothing, not even God.[64]

Awe is necessary for abiding and producing joy in our lives. Tim Keller said once, "Joy is profoundly thoughtful."[65] Thinking deeply about God's holiness, His power, His promises, and His sovereignty helps us not have a shallow faith. We don't just want to think about the things of God but *believe* them. So often, we ponder our problems more than God's providence. But, pondering God's nature and character reminds us that we are not the vinedresser nor the vine, but we are the branches. When we have awe of God, it draws us closer to God and gives us confidence in Him. As Jerry Bridges wrote, "It is a profound sense of veneration and honor, reverence and awe, that draws forth from our hearts worship, and adoration that characterizes true devotion to God"[66] As Hebrews 12:28-29 says, "let us offer to God acceptable worship, with reverence and awe, for our God is a consuming fire."

So, spend time on walks, on your couch, in bed, deeply pondering God. Read parts of the Bible you've never read before. Read books that will challenge your thinking and theology. Ask others to do it with you and discuss the deeper things together. When you do this, you'll discover that joy is found in the deeper places. As Psalm 64:9-10 says, "All people will fear; they will proclaim the works of God and *ponder* what he has done. The righteous will *rejoice* in the Lord and take refuge in him; all the upright in heart will glory in him!" (NIV).

ABIDE WITH YOUR BODY

Much of our abiding has to do with our body. Paul says in 1 Corinthians 6:19-20, "Do you not know that your body is a temple of the Holy Spirit within you, whom you have from God? You are not your own, for you were bought with a price. So glorify God in your body." Often, this verse is used to champion the idea of diet and exercise. There's always that buff brother at the gym who says, "I have to take care of this temple!" Although we are supposed to take care of our bodies, abiding is so much more. As the Holy Spirit abides in our bodies, let's explore how we can use our bodies to abide in Jesus and give Him glory.

Hands and Feet

In the seventeenth century, a French Carmelite monk named Brother Lawrence served in a monastery in Paris. He wasn't any ordinary monk who worked in the sanctuary. Instead, his sanctuary was the kitchen! Brother Lawrence was a cook for the monastery and served there for nearly his whole life. But it wasn't Brother Lawrence's stew that made him well-known; it was his love and joy for God. He learned in his walk with Jesus that no matter where you go and what you do, you do it in the presence of God. A collection of his letters and notes make up his book *The Practice of the Presence of God*. He wrote, "Thus I continued some years, applying my mind carefully to the rest of the day, and even in the midst of my business, *to the presence of God*, whom I consider always as *with* me, often as *in* me."[67]

Brother Lawrence channeled a truth found throughout all of Scripture. God's presence is always with us. This was true for Moses, Joshua, Isaiah, and others, but it is especially true for us.

Right before ascending to heaven, Jesus told His disciples and us that He is always with us to the end of the age (Matthew 28:20). This means everywhere your feet take you, Jesus is with you. So, as you go to work, to school, on a date, to the grocery store, to lunch, and to the gym, Jesus is with you. This may seem like a weird idea, as if Jesus is some kind of imaginary friend. But Jesus' presence is so real. We just have to practice being present with Him.

What can help us be present with Jesus is to do everything with Him consciously. He gave you your hands with special skills to use for His glory. It doesn't matter if your hands are calloused or smooth; He's given you your hands to create, design, write, manage, fix, or build for Him and with Him. He has experience doing those things, too, you know? Then, our work becomes an act of worship. Even in the spontaneous times of the day, He may urge you to help, serve, or give. Every day, He has prepared ahead of time good works for us to do (Ephesians 2:9-10). We just have to be willing to go where He wants us to go and do what He wants us to do. There is nothing more joyful than being used by Jesus.

We can also find joy with Jesus in ordinary tasks. As you drive kids to practice, do the laundry, make dinner, or mow the lawn, do it all with Jesus. Sometimes, these daily tasks seem daunting, and we dread doing them. But if you invite Jesus to do those things with you, the tasks you once dreaded, you now delight in because He is with you, and you are with Him. I know many of us are bogged down by our busyness and cluttered calendars. We feel like we never have time for Him and feel guilty. But Jesus doesn't want you to fit Him into your busy schedule; He wants you to be with Him in your busy schedule. You will feel connected to Him throughout the day, and His presence will give you joy. As Psalm 16:11 says, "You will fill me with *joy* in your presence."

Eyes and Ears

What do your eyes and ears dwell on most? What do you watch, look at, and listen to? As I shared in chapter five, we are constantly distracted by our devices. We're always checking notifications, scrolling social media, checking emails, texting, playing games, and watching videos. The good ole pocket slot machine! Also, in many ways, we've been desensitized by the darkness and are entertained by evil. Now, you may roll your eyes at that, thinking I'm being over dramatic. I get it. But, I believe we feel disconnected from Jesus and struggle to have joy because we're not abiding with our eyes and ears. Jesus even warned that what you consume is what you become (Matthew 6:22-23). I don't know about you, but I'd rather be shaped by the Holy Spirit instead of an algorithm.

Now, I won't tell you that you need to delete your Hulu, Netflix, or Instagram. Everyone is different and at a different place in their walk. But, I am going to challenge you to be honest and obedient to the Spirit's leading. He may lead you to delete your social media, add screen time, turn off notifications, or get a dumb phone (that's what they're called). You may need to limit your options for what you watch and listen to. But as a believer, you are called "to present your bodies as a living sacrifice, holy and acceptable to God, which is your spiritual worship." (Romans 12:1). Abiding requires sacrifice and holiness. So, lay aside anything hindering you from abiding and fix your eyes on Jesus (Hebrews 12:1-2). Okay, but how?

Obviously, reading God's Word is vital, which we have explored. Psalm 19:8 says, "The precepts of the Lord are right, *rejoicing* the heart, the commandment of the Lord is pure, enlightening the eyes." But also, we must look for Jesus in the world around us. Everything we see and hear was created by Him, through Him, and for Him (Colossians 1:6). Look at the beauty of His creation in nature. In a teaching on anxiety and worry, Jesus told His listeners to look at the birds and flowers to remind them of their value and that God cares for them (Matthew 6:25-33). What if we applied this literally? Instead of filling the void by constantly looking down at our devices, gaze at Jesus' creativity and beauty all around you. Look at the different colors and details of flowers and trees. Listen to the sound of a bird's song and the chirping of crickets. We can even see Jesus in people. The squeal of an infant's belly laugh. The warm smile of an elderly man at the grocery store. Jesus' goodness is all around us; we just need to have eyes to see and ears to hear Him. And when we do, our response is rejoicing. As Psalm 70:4 says, "May all who seek you *rejoice* and be glad in you! May those who love your salvation say evermore, "God is great!"

Tongue and Thumbs

Not too long ago, I was driving home from work and using that alone time to pray as I often do. While driving, I got cut off in traffic, which nearly caused an accident. I remember saying, "You moron! Do you know how to drive?!" Almost immediately, James 3:9-10 came to mind, which says, "With the tongue we praise our Lord and Father, and with it we curse human beings, who have been made in God's likeness. Out of the same mouth come praise and cursing. My brothers and sisters, this should not be" (NIV). Oh boy. I was convicted. At that moment, I realized I needed to make some changes. I decided to stop praying in the car!

In all seriousness, our tongue is very powerful. We can use it for God's glory, or we can use it to hurt ourselves and hurt others. Jesus says it's not what goes in the mouth that defiles a person but what comes out (Matthew 15:11). Paul instructs in Ephesians 4:29, "Let no corrupting talk come out of your mouths, but only such as is good for building up, as fits the occasion, that it may give grace to those who hear."

The word "corrupted" is the Greek word *sapros,* a rare word only used eight times in the New Testament. The other seven times it's used is to describe rotten tree fruit. So, Paul is saying, don't let rotten fruit come out of your mouth. Don't say words that stink and cause you and others to be sick. What is rotten fruit talk like? Cursing, gossip, slander, complaining, boasting, fits of rage, hateful slurs, and crude jokes (Ephesians 5:4, Romans 1:29-30, Philippians 2:14). These things don't just apply to our talking, but also our typing. Whether posting, texting, or commenting, you are serving rotten or good fruit. And Jesus says what comes out of you actually reveals the condition of your heart. Jesus said, "But what comes out of the mouth proceeds from the heart, and this defiles a person" (Matthew 15:18). In other words, what comes out of you reveals whether you're abiding in Jesus.

So, let's be aware of our words and make sure we are abiding and producing good fruit. Words that are "good for building up, as fits the occasion, that it may give grace to those who hear." (Ephesians 4:29b-d). Go through the day looking to use your words to build people up, not tear them down. Intentionally look to give people the gift of encouragement. Keep your tone always gentle and kind, even when you have to say hard things. And look for any opportunity to share the gospel. Whether it's a lost person or a seasoned believer, we all need to hear and be reminded of Jesus' grace and truth. And always give Jesus the glory, the credit, and the praise He deserves.

Lastly, we ought to sing and rejoice! A University of Oxford study showed that singing reduces stress and anxiety and produces joy![68] When we sing, it resets our minds and bodies and brings us back into alignment with God. It's no wonder why the Psalms and singing is so important in our worship. So, when you're feeling stressed out or anxious or just want to connect with God, sing worship to Him and be filled with joy! As Psalm 100:1-2 says, "Make a *joyful* noise to the Lord, all the earth! Serve the Lord with gladness! Come into his presence with singing!"

ABIDE WITH YOUR SPIRIT

As we've explored, abiding in Jesus has much to do with our mind and body, but it also has to do with our spirit. The primary way we do this is through prayer. Although praying uses our mind and body, it is especially spiritual. Prayer connects us with Jesus in a supernatural way. Paul instructs us to "*Rejoice* always, pray without ceasing, give thanks in all circumstances; for this is the will of God in Christ Jesus for you" (1 Thessalonians 5:16). For the longest time, I didn't understand what it meant to rejoice always or pray without ceasing. How am I supposed to pray all day? It just seemed unusual and unrealistic, but really, it's not. Unceasing prayer is simply having a continual conversation with Jesus throughout the day. Brother Lawrence says this continual prayer is "a habitual, silent, and secret conversation of the soul with God, which often causes me *joys* and raptures inwardly, and sometimes also outwardly." [69] Here are a few ways we can abide in unceasing prayer:

Gratitude and Thanksgiving

In college, I took a class called Principles and Practice of Prayer. My professor was Dr. Puegh, a retired pastor who taught this class purely because he was passionate about teaching young people how to pray. Dr. Puegh was one of the most joyful men I knew, and I was eager to learn from him.

One of the first things we learned was thanksgiving. In Scripture, thanksgiving is a vital part of worship and prayer (Psalms 100, 1 Thessalonians 5:16, Philippians 4:6). Typically, thanksgiving and gratitude are synonymous, but they are slightly different. Gratitude is a general appreciation, whereas thanksgiving is a personal appreciation. For example, you can be grateful for a delicious meal, but being thankful is thanking your friend for making it for you. With Jesus, we can have a sense of gratitude for our lives, but we should practice thanksgiving by personally thanking Him for specific things. I highlight that because people can be grateful for their lives, but not thankful towards God. And if we don't intentionally thank God, then we resemble an unbeliever who doesn't worship God at all (Romans 1:21). So, thanksgiving is vital to our relationship with God and our joy. How I like to think of it is if joy is a fire, then thanksgiving is the fuel.

To put thanksgiving into practice, Dr. Puegh's first assignment was to write down one hundred things we were thankful for. Yes, one hundred. Initially, the assignment seemed intimidating and daunting, but it completely changed my approach to thanksgiving. I learned that thanksgiving shouldn't be shallow; it should be specific. The assignment forced me out of the shallow "Thank you, Jesus, for this day," "Thank you, Jesus, for this food," or "Thank you, Jesus, for this beautiful weather." Instead, I learned to be specific. "Thank you, Jesus, for my friend Trooper who loves you." "Thank you, Jesus, for this car that has A/C." "Thank you, Jesus, for this clean water." When you do this, you start to view everything as a gift from God because it all is (James 1:7).

As Dr. Puegh gave me that assignment many years ago, I give the same assignment to you! Yes, write or type out one hundred things you are thankful for. There's no deadline, obviously, but set a deadline for yourself so you'll be motivated to complete it. Then keep it. Don't throw it away. You'll enjoy reading it in the future, I promise.

Thanksgiving is a great exercise, but it needs to be a daily discipline. How detailed you are in your one hundred things; you should be as detailed every day in thanking Jesus. Practically, you can do this in different ways. Some of my dear friends write down at least three things they are thankful for each morning or night. Or, as you go throughout the day, you can continually stop and thank Him for specific things. The more intentionally you look for His work and thank Him for it, the more you'll find joy in small and simple things that are often overlooked or taken for granted. We all have reasons to rejoice always; we just have to be aware and thank Him for all of it.

Confess and Repent

One time, when I came home from work, I noticed something peculiar on one of the walls by our kitchen. After closer examination, I realized it was an incredible color pencil masterpiece Ellie drew. We're talking all over the wall. So, I find Ellie and ask her, "Ellie, why did you draw on the wall?" She responded, "I didn't, Daddy. I think Hank did it." Hank is our cat. I was shocked, to say the least. I didn't know he was such a skilled artist.

As funny and cute as this was, the question is, why did Ellie respond that way? Samantha and I didn't teach Ellie to lie, deny wrongdoing, or blame someone else (or a cat) for her actions. Where did she learn that? The answer is she didn't learn it. Rather, it's her nature, and it's our nature as well.

When we sin, our default is to hide, cover up, act like it's no big deal, pretend it didn't happen, or blame someone else. Thinking back to the Garden in Genesis 3, that's exactly what Adam and Eve did. After they sinned, they covered up, hid from God, and blamed each other. That broke God's heart and still breaks God's heart when we do the same. If we are to abide in Jesus, what we need to do is not conceal our sin but rather confess it. As Proverbs 28:13 says, "Whoever conceals their sins does not prosper, but the one who confesses and renounces them finds mercy" (NIV).

When we sin, we sin against God, and sin is personal. After Nathan confronted David about his adultery with Bathsheba, he wrote Psalm 51, a prayer of repentance. In Psalm 51:4, he says, "Against you, you only, have I sinned and done what is evil in your sight." Like David, when we confess our sins to Jesus, we take responsibility and ask for forgiveness.

We don't want unconfessed sin to disconnect us from Him. So we say, "Jesus, I'm so sorry I reacted that way, or watched that, or took that, or thought that." And when we are faithful to confess, He is faithful to forgive. 1 John 1:9 says, "If we confess our sins, he is faithful and just to forgive us our sins and to cleanse us from all unrighteousness."

Practically, if I were to coach you on confession, I would encourage you to confess in the moment. After you dwell on something, your eyes linger, you have an angry outburst, you exaggerate something, or you pursue an idol instead of Jesus, right then confess to Him. "Lord, I'm so sorry; help me not do that again." This practice is helpful because it makes you more aware of your sin. Most days, we sin without even thinking twice. So, if you are more aware of your sin, confess it, and ask for help to repent, you'll notice the Holy Spirit changing your heart. Confession changes callused hearts and keeps us deeply connected to Jesus. Then He will restore the joy of your salvation (Psalm 51:12).

Petition and Submission

What do you typically ask God for? From my experience and observation, we usually ask God for good health. Or we ask for healing if we or someone else are sick or suffering. We often ask for protection and safety as friends and family travel. We also ask God to provide for our needs, such as jobs and finances.

Asking God for things is good, and it's encouraged. As Paul says in Philippians 4:6, "Do not be anxious about anything, but in every situation, by prayer and petition, with thanksgiving, present your requests to God."

But, our prayer life can become stagnant if all we do is ask Jesus for things, approaching Him like a genie who exists to serve us. This approach is especially true when we have the wrong motives. James 4:3 says, "When you ask, you do not receive, because you ask with wrong motives, that you may spend what you get on your pleasures" (NIV). Sometimes, we ask Jesus for things that are actually feeding our worldly idols. For example, someone may pray for a raise or promotion at work, but they are asking because they want to upgrade their lifestyle, feeding their idols of money, possessions, achievement, or career. Then, when Jesus doesn't answer that prayer, they get upset. But Jesus will never help us feed our worship of an idol. So, when you pray, make sure there is no idol behind your request because Jesus won't answer that prayer. He doesn't exist to serve us; we exist to serve Him.

Even if your requests have pure motives, Jesus is Lord, and He gets to decide how He will answer them. When we abide in Jesus, submission follows petition. I heard someone once say, "If the motive is wrong, Jesus will say no. If the timing isn't right, Jesus will say take it slow. If you are not ready, Jesus will say you need to grow. But if the request is right, the timing is right, and you are ready, Jesus will say go!" Whether we're in the no, slow, grow, or go, we must trust and submit to Him. Because Jesus knows your heart, He knows your future, and He knows what's best. I love what Tim Keller says, "God will either give us what we ask or give us what we would have asked if we knew everything he knew."[70]

Even though most of our prayer requests involve asking Jesus for things, we should also practice asking Him for help. As you go through your day, along with your thanksgiving and confession, you should ask Jesus to help you in everything you do. Ask Him to help you with decisions, writing emails, or navigating tough conversations. Ask Him to help you not have lingering eyes, dwell on negative thoughts, or lash out in anger. Ask Him to help you abide.

Naturally, we ask Jesus for help in areas of weakness, but you should also ask Him in areas of strength. Otherwise, pride settles in our hearts, thinking we don't need Jesus, but we do. When we ask for help, we humble ourselves before Him and put ourselves in a position to live in His power and wisdom, not our own. This is a vital part of exercising our dependence and abiding in Him. Then, when Jesus answers our prayers, we have so much joy! As Jesus said in John 16:23-24, "Truly, truly, I say to you, whatever you ask of the Father in my name, he will give it to you. Until now, you have asked nothing in my name. Ask, and you will receive that your *joy* may be full."

Rest and Recover

Remember when we had scheduled nap times? It's been a minute for some of us, but honestly, we should bring them back. Who's with me? For children, daily scheduled naps and rest times are necessary for development. When children get out of routine and don't rest, they become monsters. I have two of those. We have to fight to stay in routine. And guess what? As adults, we're not that different. Just like children need a rhythm of rest for their development, we need a rhythm of rest to abide in Jesus.

God designed us to have a rhythm of rest in our lives, weekly and daily. After God created the whole universe in six days, He rested on the seventh day and made it holy. He called this day the Sabbath, the Hebrew word *Shabbat*, which means "to stop" and "to delight." John Mark Comer wrote that the Sabbath "has a dual idea of stopping and also joying in God and our lives in his world. The Sabbath is an entire day set aside to follow God's example, to stop and delight."[71] The author of Hebrews says, "for whoever has entered God's rest has also rested from his works as God did from his. Let us therefore strive to enter that rest" (Hebrews 4:10-11).

So, how do we Sabbath? Pick one day a week (it doesn't have to be Sunday) when you "stop" any work. No emails. No labor. No fixing. No writing. No meetings. Do everything you can to protect your day off. Then, "delight" in God by intentionally spending extra intimate time with Him. Slow down, read, meditate, pray, and do things you enjoy with Him. What are your hobbies? What do you like to do that is life-giving and fun? The advice given to me is to do something that is the opposite of your job and that you really enjoy. During the week, I use my mind to speak and type a lot. On my sabbath day (Friday), I do yard work and grill, which I enjoy. John Mark Comer presents a question to consider, "what could I do for twenty-four hours that would fill my soul with deep, throbbing *joy*? That would make me spontaneously combust with wonder, awe, gratitude, and praise?"[72] Think about your answer to that question. Then, do it!

In addition to our weekly rest, we need daily rest as well. We think our lives are busy, but Jesus was busy, too. He constantly traveled from town to town, managing and teaching His disciples. He would teach to crowds all morning at the synagogues and heal people all day into the evenings. But, even though Jesus was busy, He knew when to stop and rest. Jesus prioritized alone time before and after His work. Mark 1:35 says, "And rising very early in the morning, while it was still dark, he departed and went out to a desolate place, and there he prayed." Then, when large crowds needed Him for healing, "he would withdraw to desolate places and pray" (Luke 5:16). Think about it: Jesus didn't heal every person who needed Him. He said no to people when it was time to stop and rest. We need to do the same. People are always going to "need you," but what you need to do is rest. Whatever it is, 99% of the time, it can wait.

Also, notice that Jesus would go to "desolate places." Sometimes, it was a garden, mountain, or desert. He didn't go back to His tent to play games with Peter. Instead, He went to be with the Father and pray. There is a reason Jesus did this. Our lives are loud and disruptive. To connect with God deeply, we have to get on His frequency through silence and solitude. This is a great time to pray and take a few moments to sit and say nothing. Just be still in His presence, and maybe you'll hear His still small whisper in your heart. What can be your desolate place?

When we rest, we need to make sure we are actually resting. It's okay to enjoy a show and eat ice cream, but don't do it till late into the night. It's important to have a consistent bedtime at a reasonable hour and consistently wake up at the same time in the morning. Remember, we thrive in rhythms of rest. In bed, put the screens away and fight against the urge to scroll. Also, don't work before bed. Replace those times with spiritual practices that we've explored in this chapter. The goal of abiding is that you would enjoy Jesus from the beginning until the end of the day. Remember, abiding is a walk, not a sprint. What's one step you can take with Him?

REFLECTION AND DISCUSSION QUESTIONS

1. In what ways do you abide well? List your top three.
2. In what ways do you not abide so well? List your top three.
3. Of the different ways to abide, what do you think will be the most challenging for you? And why?
4. Of the different ways to abide, what are you most excited to start doing?
5. At what times and places do you feel closest to Jesus? Why do you think that is?
6. In what ways can you add people to your abiding?

CHAPTER SEVEN

Joy Thieves

I'm not sure if you've ever heard of Shohei Ohtani, but he is the greatest baseball player on the planet right now. He is a unique "two-way" player, which means he pitches and hits. If you're not a baseball person, that's a big deal. Normally, you're either a pitcher or a hitter. Rarely does one player do both. Not only does Ohtani hit and pitch, but when he's healthy, he's also the best in the league in both categories. Basically, Ohtani is worth the equivalent of two All-Star players in one. That's why he earned a record 10-year, $700-million contract with the Los Angeles Dodgers in 2024.[73] That contract makes him the second highest-paid player in North American sports history. Crazy, right? But Ohtani's phenomenal baseball skills and monster contract aren't the only reason he was in the headlines in 2024.

Ohtani is Japanese and doesn't speak or understand English well. Since joining the league in 2018, Ohtani has had an interpreter and long-time friend, Ippei Mizuhara. Everywhere

Ohtani went, Mizuhara went. He was there for every game in every city. He was Ohtani's ears and mouth but also a companion in a foreign land.

In the Spring of 2024, news broke that Mizuhara had been stealing from Ohtani for the last three years to cover sports gambling debts. Over that period, Mizuhara stole over $17 million. I can't imagine that. I'd be upset if someone stole just $10 from me. For Ohtani, he was shocked and hurt deeply to learn this. His long-time friend had been stealing from him, and he didn't know it. He felt betrayed and embarrassed. Today, Mizuhara is in jail, and Ohtani has a new interpreter.

Now, you may not have millions of dollars stolen from you, but there are things that are stealing your joy. I call these "Joy Thieves." In chapter five, I covered joy idols, which are things we actively pursue to give us joy. But joy thieves are not things we pursue. They are things that steal our joy that we are oblivious to. And as you'll see, all of our joy thieves have to do with our relationships with others.

Remember, joy is a supernatural emotion empowered by the Holy Spirit when we are deeply connected to Jesus and others. We've explored in the previous chapters how we can be deeply connected to Jesus, but another piece that is vital to our joy is being deeply connected to others. As we explored in the previous two chapters, if you lack joy in your life, it's likely a connection problem. Just like we may have a connection problem with Jesus, we may also have a connection problem with people. Which studies show we likely do.

In general, we have a major connection problem today. I shared in chapter three that in 2023, the Surgeon General of the U.S., Vivek Murthy, wrote a research article titled "Our Epidemic of Loneliness and Isolation." For clarity moving forward, here are two definitions of isolation and loneliness:

Isolation - *is to be alone.* Isolation means there are no people around. Think back to Covid, when we had to isolate in quarantine to prevent the spread of the virus. Or, when you got in trouble at home, you would be sent to your room. Or, if someone breaks a serious law in our land, they can be sentenced to prison, isolating them from society. Even in prison, the worst punishment apart from the death penalty is what? Solitary confinement. Isolation is often a punishment in our day.

Loneliness - *is the feeling of being alone even if you're not.* You can be in proximity to people but feel as if you're all alone. You may feel unnoticed when you're around people, as if you are invisible. You often feel left out in social environments or don't have close friends or meaningful relationships. You feel like no one cares about you. You can feel this way at work, school, church, family, or even in a marriage. There's proximity but no intimacy.

According to the study, approximately half of U.S. adults report experiencing loneliness, with some of the highest rates among young adults. This study found that loneliness is as dangerous as smoking fifteen cigarettes a day. Loneliness increases the risk of premature death by 29%, with the leading cause being heart disease.[74] Yes, being lonely hurts your heart. Why is this?

When God completed each day of His creation, the Bible says it was good. The sky, the water, the land, the stars, the plants, the animals, even man was all good. But, after creating all the good things, God looked at Adam and said, "It is *not good* for man to be *alone*" (Genesis 2:18). Then, God created Eve. Now, when God said this, He was not speaking just about marriage; He was speaking about our *design*. We are designed for relationships, and without them, we suffer and get sick.

For the remainder of this chapter, we will explore what disconnects us from people and makes us isolated and lonely. These are our joy thieves. We'll learn how these things steal our joy, how to stop them, and how to get our joy back.

Our Screens

So far in this book, I've presented how our devices can disconnect us from God. But our devices can also disconnect us from people. That is not my opinion; studies show it. The American Time Use Survey revealed that there has been a significant shift in how much time we spend with friends in the last twenty years. The survey showed:

> 20 Years Ago = 30 Hours Per Month with Friends (7.5 Hours a week)
> Today = 10 Hours Per Month with Friends (2.5 Hours a week)[75]

As you can see, the amount of time spent with friends has significantly declined in the last twenty years. What's interesting is that the numbers nosedived in 2008. You might wonder, what happened in 2008? Well, that's when smartphones came to market. That's when our phone became our friend.

Our phones offer communication and community without the risks of true relationships.

Texting, group chats, gaming servers, and social media are tools to stay in touch with people, but they can't be our primary place for connection because they are insufficient. You can communicate information but can't connect emotionally, which is needed. It's like we are all starving for connection, and we snack on our phones, thinking we're getting plenty to eat, but in reality, we're still starving. Have you ever considered why social media is called a "feed?" We are ever communicating but never satisfied or full. Our phones are making us isolated and lonely.

The *American Journal of Preventive Medicine* conducted a study that found participants who used social media for more than two hours a day were roughly twice as likely to report feeling socially isolated compared to those who spent less than 30 minutes on these platforms daily.[76] So, if you are looking for guidelines for how much social media you should have per day, this study shows a good benchmark. Limit your social media use to at least 30 minutes and see what happens.

But it's not just about replacing time with people with our phones. Even when we are with people, we are on our phones. Not too long ago, I was in our playroom with Ellie doing a puzzle. While doing the puzzle, I was responding to emails on my phone. Ellie asked me, "What are you looking at, Daddy?" Then it hit me: I was looking at my phone more than I was looking at my daughter. That's a serious issue. But I know I'm not alone. When we are on our phones around people, we may be communicating on our phones, but we're also communicating to the people around us that they are less important. Even though we are present, we're really not present. That severely disconnects us from the people we love most.

So, keep your phone in your pocket or leave it in another room when you're with people. If you're sharing a meal, don't even put it on the table. The time you spend with family and friends is more important than what you will look at. Also, start a conversation instead of filling the void with a screen. Ask questions, especially fun questions! "Would you rather questions" are gold. Get to know one another and have fun with it. Or play games. Or make up a game! You can do a lot with duct tape and toilet paper. Just saying. Here's the thing: Boredom is not a joy thief; it's an opportunity for conversation and creativity, which leads to deeper connections and joy.

You should also take this approach in public. When we're out in places, the social norm is to pull out our phones, scroll social media, check emails, check the weather, or whatever, just to avoid awkward interactions with strangers. Our phones are modern-day adult security blankets. But this, yet again, is a joy thief. A University of British Columbia study found that putting phones away and talking to strangers actually gives people joy.[77] No, the study group wasn't just extroverts. The study found that people felt more connected to their community, which gave them joy. Ah, yes. Joy is all about connection. So, you want to have joy? Talk to strangers! Seriously, try it. Phone away. Eyes up. Smile big!

What about online church? It depends. Online church is good on occasion when you're traveling or sick. But, it also provides a convenient and comfortable option, which does become a problem. Online church can't be your primary because you can't fully connect with others. Technology is a good tool, but face-to-face fellowship is necessary. 2 John 12 says, "Though

I have much to write to you, I would rather not use paper and ink. Instead, I hope to come to you and talk face-to-face so that our *joy* may be complete." Tony Reinke says, "Joy brings our attention, our minds, and our flesh and blood together into face-to-face fellowship — eyeball-to-eyeball love. The Christian's challenge is to love not in tweets and texts only, but even more in deeds and physical presence."[78] In other words, joy is incomplete in isolation but complete in community.

Our Critic

A few years ago, I was meeting with a Christian counselor. As I shared in previous chapters, I was dealing with serious anxiety and panic attacks. While working together, he revealed something in me that is also a reality for many people today. He shared that most people have what's called the "Critic." It's not a condition (we're not crazy), but it's the negative thoughts you battle with daily. Your Critic is a collection of negative voices and experiences you've had throughout your life. Think about the times you've had harsh criticism, been made fun of, had embarrassing failures, or had traumatic experiences. All these things have been collected in your mind over time and created your Critic. In other words, your mind is a jerk and often steals your joy. This is how:

Your Critic makes you overthink everything. When you're texting, it takes you forever because you have to craft it perfectly. You think, "What if they take this the wrong way?" Or, when you're with people, your Critic will say, "Don't say that; they'll think you're dumb." Or when you pick out your outfit, you change it ten times because you think, "What are others going to think of me?" Your Critic will say, "That doesn't look good on you," or even worse, "You're just ugly." Decisions are never easy, and your Critic makes you second-guess everything.

Your Critic only points out the negative. You could have done something great; one person says something you perceive as negative, and that's all you think about. Your Critic says, "You're not good enough," or "Why do you even try?" or "You should just quit." Sometimes, even when you mess something up, you'll say aloud what you hear from your Critic. You'll accidentally do something and say, "You idiot!" or "What are you doing? Stupid!" Because of this, you're unable to enjoy the victories, successes, and positives because you only dwell on the negative.

Your Critic makes you assume the worst. For example, if someone hasn't talked to you in a while or acts oddly around you, your Critic will say, "You did something wrong," or "They're mad at you," or "They must not like you." Or when you want to invite someone to hang out, your Critic will say, "They're going to reject you" or "They don't want to be your friend." Your Critic will catastrophes everything and feed your anxiety.

Your Critic reminds you of your failures. Your Critic will never let you forget your failures. Rather, it reminds you often of them. Your Critic will say, "Remember what happened last time? It's going to happen again." Even in our moral failures with our sin, our Critic will say, "Remember when you watched that, said that, thought that, or did that?" "What if people found out? They're going to judge you." Your Critic chains you to the past, making you fearful and ashamed.

Your Critic will make you a people pleaser. We want people to like us, but our Critic says, "No one will like you for who you are." So, we become a people pleaser, which is like a chameleon. We do whatever everyone else likes because we want to blend in. But, in doing so, no one really gets to know you. Also, you feel like you can never say no when people ask you to do things. Your Critic will say, "You're letting them down," or "You're a terrible friend if you don't do this." When you people please, you lose who you are, and no one really knows who you are.

Overall, your Critic makes you think horrible things about yourself. It makes you think you're bad at your job, you're a horrible parent, terrible spouse, a lousy friend, and an awful Christ follower. Most of us believe our Critic, and because we do, we isolate ourselves; we're quiet, reserved, disconnected, afraid of people, and feel very lonely. Satan uses our Critic to control us and make us feel like we're alone, and many times he is successful. We need to stop listening to our Critic and start listening to our *Creator*.

- Your Critic says you are not good enough; your Creator says Jesus was enough (Hebrews 10:14).
- Your Critic says you're a failure; your Creator says you're not defined by your failures (1 John 3:20).
- Your Critic says you're ugly; your Creator says you're beautifully and wonderfully made. (Psalm 139:14).
- Your Critic says you're worthless; your Creator says you were worth dying for (Romans 5:8).
- Your Critic says your life is out of control; your Creator says I'm in control (Proverbs 19:21).
- Your Critic says you're not loved; your Creator says I'll never stop loving you (Romans 8:1).

- Your Critic says no one cares; your Creator says I care more for you than anything else in the world (1 Peter 5:7).
- Your Critic says you're alone; your Creator says you're never alone (Matthew 28:20)

We must take every thought captive and make it obedient to Christ. Don't let your Critic drive your life and decisions and steal your joy. It's a liar and makes you lonely. Instead, listen to the voice of your Lord (John 10:27). Be kind to yourself. Give yourself grace. Love yourself the way Jesus loves you.

Our Comparison

Have you heard the saying, "Comparison is the thief of joy"? You may think that's a Bible verse or a quote from some famous theologian or ancient monk. But it was said by our 26th U.S. President, Theodore Roosevelt![79] Even though the phrase is not in the Bible, the principle is. The question is, what are we comparing that is stealing our joy?

First, I'd like to point out that not all comparison is bad. Comparison is good in the context of discipleship. We should constantly compare our lives to Jesus to become more like Him. Even Paul called his followers to compare and imitate him, as he compared and imitated Christ (1 Corinthians 11:1). Even today, it's wise to compare our lives to mature believers and imitate their lives. But outside of discipleship, comparison is destructive.

We often compare ourselves to people on social media. This makes us depressed because our lives don't measure up to their beauty, money, and fame. We also compare ourselves to others who are closest to us. We are constantly comparing, whether it's family, friends, co-workers, neighbors, or someone at church.

We compare what people wear, the cars we drive, the size of our houses, the jobs we have, how much money we make, and so on. Our comparison makes us envious of others. Then, our comparison turns into a competition. Whatever others have, you want it, and you want more, and you want better.

We also compare ourselves to others to make us feel better about ourselves. We look down on others because of how they look, talk, or act. We judge people and distance ourselves from them because we think we're better than them. But this is wrong. Jesus says in Matthew 7:1-2, "Judge not, that you be not judged. For with the judgment you pronounce, you will be judged, and with the measure you use, it will be measured to you." Keeping with the presidents, George W. Bush once said, "Too often, we judge others by their worst examples - while judging ourselves by our best intentions. And this has strained our bonds of understanding and common purpose."[80] When you do this, you do not love your neighbor.

So, what do we do? First, we need to stop competing with one another. Galatians 6:4 says "Each one should test their own actions. Then they can take pride in themselves alone, without comparing themselves to someone else" (NIV). Paul makes it clear that we shouldn't compare ourselves to others. Rather, we should focus on our work, blessings, and giftings. Be content with what the Lord has given you. Competition has its place but doesn't have a place in community, except for Pickleball. That's fun competition!

Second, instead of comparing ourselves to people, we must look at them compassionately. When Jesus looked at people who were rich and poor, clean and dirty, He didn't compare Himself, thinking He was better than them. Rather, He looked at them with compassion, knowing they all needed Him desperately (Matthew 9:36). Compassion leads to action. Spend time with them, get to know them, hear their stories, serve them, and love them well.

In Matthew 7, Jesus says that the measurement that we judge, we will be judged. The way we measure ourselves and others is wrong. When other people are the measurement (I can't measure up to them), we become discouraged and jealous. When we are the measurement (they can't measure up to me), we become conceited and judgmental. But, when Jesus is the measurement, He evens the playing field because we're all sinners and need grace. So, how are you measuring? Because it's impossible to be joyful, jealous, and judgmental at the same time.

Our Complaining

Do you complain a lot? Complaining is something we all struggle with. We often complain because things don't go the way we planned, we have unmet expectations, or something takes longer than it should, and we are impatient. When these things happen, we easily get frustrated and annoyed and complain. Complaining is very easy, but it costs us so much. Without even realizing it, our complaining is stealing our joy.

Three days after God saved Israel from Egypt, the people complained to Moses because there wasn't clean water to drink (Exodus 15:24). Seriously? After 400 years of slavery, ten plagues, and miraculously parting the Red Sea to escape, they complained because they were thirsty? Less than a month later, the people complained to Moses again because they were hungry and wished they had stayed in Egypt (Exodus 16:2-3). Really? What is wrong with these people? They were complainers. They were ungrateful and forgetful of what God had done for them. Complaining blinded them from God's goodness. All they could see was what they lacked instead of what they had. Now, we can point the finger at Israel, but we are guilty of this as well.

Our complaining affects us, but it affects other people, too. As we unpacked an abiding tongue, complaining is rotten fruit and makes you and others sick. When Jon Gordon wrote his book *Energy Bus*, he wrote about "Energy Vampires."[81] An Energy Vampire is someone who is constantly negative and a chronic complainer. People don't want to be around energy vampires because they bring everyone down around them. When we complain, we're not just an energy vampire but joy vampires. When we complain, we suck the joy out of ourselves and others with our negativity, discontentment, and entitlement.

The Bible is clear that complaining is a sin. Paul says in Philippians 2:14, "Do all things without grumbling or disputing." Specifically, James commands us not to complain about others (James 5:9), and Peter commands us not to complain when we serve others (1 Peter 4:9). In a way, the Bible commands a "no-complaining rule" for all believers.

When Mike Smith was the head coach of the Atlanta Falcons, they had a no-complaining rule. They even made wristbands that said, "No Complaining."[82] The team bought in, and it brought their team closer together. They kept each other accountable to make sure no one complained. This team bonding translated into incredible success, making it to Super

Bowl LI. So, the no-complaining rule is proven to be great for teams, but it's also a great rule for life. It can be a rule of life for yourself, but you can even make it a rule in your family, friends, small group, and so on. See what happens. Just imagine what your life would look like if you stopped complaining. I'd imagine it would be more joyful.

Now, there is such a thing as righteous complaining. When there is injustice or dealing with grief, complaining can be warranted. This is much different than Starbucks taking too long to make your latte. When David was dealing with the injustice of his enemies, he wrote, "Here my voice, O God, in my *complaint*; preserve my life from dread of the enemy" (Psalm 64:1). But, notice *who* David brings his complaint to. He brings his complaint to God in prayer. When you have a righteous complaint, make sure you direct it to Him.

Also, instead of just stopping our complaining, we should replace our complaining with prayer. What does that look like? Here are some examples.

> **Complaint:** "Ugh, I hate when it rains."
> **Prayer:** "God, thank you for the rain and how it nourishes our land."

> **Complaint:** "Man, I can't stand working with that guy."
> **Prayer:** "God, thank you for my job and the people I work with. I pray for my coworker that he would know you and have a blessed day. Please help me love him well."

Complaint: "I'm so tired of being sick! Why does this keep happening?!"
Prayer: God, thank you for life. Thank you for the medicine and doctors you have blessed me with to help me. Please help me use this extra time of rest to spend with you. Please heal my body."

This practice of prayer turns entitlement to thanksgiving, frustration to faithfulness, impatient to patient, joyless to joyful. It's impossible to rejoice when you complain, and it's impossible to complain when you rejoice. Don't be a joy vampire.

Our Unforgiveness

I don't have to know you to know that people have hurt you. We've all been hurt by others in some way, from big to small, from complete strangers to the people closest to us. Sometimes, it was what they did to you. They said something hurtful to your face or behind your back. They lied to you or betrayed you in some way. Or, in serious cases, they physically harmed you.

Or, sometimes, it's what they didn't do. They didn't go to your games or performances. They weren't there for you when you needed them the most. They were physically not present, or maybe they were emotionally unavailable. Or, they didn't invite, acknowledge, or include you, so you felt left out.

No matter the case, people hurt us, intentionally or unintentionally. And if we're being honest, we hurt other people, too. But it's not the hurt that is a joy thief; it's our unforgiveness.

When we get hurt, our default is to isolate. We stop hanging out. We stop talking. We stop coming to our small group.

We stop coming to church. We feel like we can't trust anyone anymore. We feel like no one cares. So, we dwell on it, and we hurt alone. But that's not helpful; it's harmful.

Deion Sanders was a Hall of Fame football player (and played baseball) and is now the current head football coach at the University of Colorado. In his first season at Colorado, many reporters and other coaches talked badly about his program and him personally. In a press conference, Deion said, *"I keep receipts."*[83] That's competitive talk, meaning I know who you are and what you said, and you'll pay for that on the field. Now, I love that as a sports fan. But the more I think about it, we keep receipts, too, don't we?

We keep receipts in our minds and hearts of when people hurt us. When we're around the person or when we think of them, we think, "You owe me." You owe me an apology. You owe me money. We want them to feel bad for what they did to us. In a darker reality, we want them to hurt the way they hurt us. We want them to pay for what they did. So, we hold on to the receipt, turning our hearts bitter in isolation. But holding a grudge won't help anything, but turning to Jesus will. And what He'll do is command you and coach you to forgive.

In Matthew 18, Jesus taught His disciples about forgiveness, using a parable about a master and his servant. The servant had a debt he could not pay (estimation in the billions). So, instead of setting up a payment plan or coming up with some kind of retribution, the master, out of his grace and kindness, forgave the servant of all his debt and let him go free! How incredible! Well, that same servant had a co-worker who owed him money, and he shook him down, demanding he pay him back. Word got back to master, and he was furious. He had the servant thrown in jail and demanded repayment. Jesus finished the parable by saying, "This is how my heavenly Father will treat each of you unless you forgive your brother or sister from your heart" (NIV).

We must forgive because we have been forgiven (Ephesians 4:32). God is the only one who rightfully and righteously keeps receipt of everyone's sins. And we should not keep receipts because Jesus paid our receipts. Love does not keep a record of wrongs (1 Corinthians 13:5). If you are not willing to forgive, then you don't have a right understanding of how much you've been forgiven. Unforgiveness only hurts yourself, but forgiveness will set you free. As Max Lucado once said, "Forgiveness is unlocking the door to set someone free and realizing you were the prisoner!"[84]

Okay, so how do we forgive? First, don't hold their wrongdoing over them. Forgiveness is saying in your heart that they don't owe you anything. They don't need to apologize or feel bad, and you don't need revenge. Leave justice to Jesus and let go of their debt. Choose not to replay the offense in your mind. Any time you think about them or the hurt, give it to Jesus. Ask Him to help you forgive. Forgiveness is hard, and that's why we need to abide in Him.

Second, if it's possible, talk it out. A conversation is not necessary for forgiveness, but it is for the relationship. Jesus says in Matthew 18:15, "If your brother sins against you, go and tell him his fault, between you and him alone." Too often, we go to other people instead of the person who hurt us. That is an unbiblical practice, and it's hurting the church. So, go to the person and tell them how they hurt you. "You hurt me by _____" or "You hurt me when _____." They may respond well, or they might not. But no matter the outcome, you must still forgive. Then your heart can be free, and your joy can be restored. So, who do you need to forgive?

Our Secrets

Do you have any secrets? Columbia University says most people do. They conducted a study that found "on average, people have about 13 secrets at any one time, five of which they have never told another person."[85] Now, some information you should keep secret, such as your social security and bank information. But most of the time, our secrets are things we've done in the past that we're ashamed of. Things you've vowed never to tell anyone, and you are committed to take it to the grave. Or they are secret sins that you don't want your spouse, friends, family, or co-workers to know about. These are your secrets that are stealing your joy.

In the previous chapter, we discussed the importance of confessing our sin instead of concealing it. We confess our sins to Jesus to be in the right relationship with Him. But Scripture also commands believers to confess their sins to one another. James 5:16 says, "Therefore, confess your sins to one another and pray for one another, that you may be healed. The prayer of a righteous person has great power as it is working." In other words, we confess our sins to Jesus to be *forgiven*, and we confess our sins to one another to be *healed*. Healed from what? From the power that sin has over you. When you confess sin to others, they will pray for you and help you overcome it. But as long as your sin is hidden, it has control over you, and you're not free. The problem today is that most of us aren't healed; we're still hiding.

Why do we hide? *Fear.* We're afraid of what others will think. We're afraid of the consequences if we confess. We're afraid of being judged by others and losing friends and possibly family. We feel like we are the only ones who are struggling. So we hide and silently suffer in our prison of shame. Unconfessed sin isolates us and disconnects us from people. A paranoid, guilty conscience is incapable of having joy. But this isn't just an individual issue; it's a church issue.

Paul in Romans 12:9 says, "Let love be genuine." The Greek word for "genuine" is *anhupokritos,* which literally means "anti-hypocrite." The Christian Standard Bible renders this verse: "Let love be without hypocrisy." Today, we use hypocrite to describe someone who says something and does the opposite. But in the Greco-Roman world, a hypocrite was the same word for an *actor.* In the first century, theater performances didn't have elaborate stages or extravagant costumes, but the actors would use different masks to depict different characters. A hypocrite is meant to be "one who wears masks." So, what Paul is saying is, "Love one another without wearing masks."

Unfortunately, the church has become a stage where people perform and wear masks. We come to church and act like everything is okay, while inwardly, we are burdened and struggling. This is fake love, and fake love creates fake friends, which produces isolation and loneliness. When we wear masks, we can't genuinely love others, and others can't genuinely love us. We don't know each other. We just know each other's masks. This has to change. Our churches, small groups, families, and friends must be no-mask zones to love one another truly. We must have a culture of confession.

Otherwise, we're just performing for people instead of transforming with people.

Friend, you will never have joy wearing a mask. As Proverbs 28:13 says, "Whoever conceals their sins does not prosper, but the one who confesses and renounces them finds mercy." Jesus also says in Luke 8:17, "For nothing is hidden that will not be made manifest, nor is anything secret that will not be known and come to light." You may feel like you're alone, but you're not alone. I challenge you to bring your sins and secrets to the light. Is it hard? Yes. Will people be upset? Maybe. Is it worth it? 100%. You will be finally free and fully known. Your relationships will go deeper than ever, producing a joy you've likely never experienced. Joy comes from living in the light. So, what mask are you wearing that you need to throw away?

Our Pride

Ty Cobb was a Hall of Fame baseball player (played from 1905 to 1928) and was arguably the greatest hitter ever to live. He held 90 baseball records for half a century and still has the record for the highest career batting average (.366) and number of batting titles (12). Cobb was a great baseball player but not a great teammate. At the end of his life, right before he died, Cobb said, "I do indeed think I would have done some things differently. And if I had, I believe I would have had more friends."[86] After he died, only three past teammates showed up to his funeral. That's not even enough people to carry his casket. Ty Cobb won in baseball, but he lost in life.

You may not be a Hall of Fame baseball player, but pride will still steal your joy. Pride isolates and makes you lonely. Pride can take on many different forms in our lives. As C.J. Mahaney wrote, "The real issue here is not *if* pride exists in your heart; it's *where* pride exists and *how* pride is being expressed in your life."[87] With that in mind, consider these questions:

Do you struggle to ask for help? I sure do. I'm the guy who gets lost in Home Dept because I refuse to ask for help. But it's not just Home Dept. I struggle to ask for help in all areas of my life, and I know many of us do. Even when someone offers help, we often reject it. It goes like, "Hey, can I help?" then the common response is, "No, I got it. Thanks, though." Translation: *I don't need you.* The truth is, if you do not ask for help or reject help when it's offered, you will become lonely. Because there will be a day when you'll need help, and no one will be there—woe to the person who falls and has no one to pick him up (Ecclesiastes 4:10).

Do you struggle to serve others? You may be unwilling to serve others when it's inconvenient or undesirable. You may feel like you are above certain tasks or serving opportunities. Think about the last time someone asked for help moving, asked for help in preschool ministry, or helped with cleaning up after an event. Often, our default isn't to be eager to serve but to look for an escape plan of excuses. This is because we selfishly only want to do what's best for ourselves and not others. But in order to follow Jesus, we must humble ourselves and become servants of all (Matthew 20:26).

Do you struggle to ask or receive advice? Many of us do whatever we think is right without seeking the counsel of others. Think about the last time you made a big purchase, changed jobs, or started a relationship. You may think, "I'm an adult; I can make my own decisions." But the Proverbs warn against this prideful thinking. Proverbs 12:15 says, "The way of a fool is right in his own eyes, but a wise man listens to advice." Our decisions in life can either bring us closer to others or distance ourselves from them.

Do you like to talk about yourself? When you're in social environments, especially meeting new people, do you like to talk about all your achievements and adventures and how awesome you are? Well, that's not awesome; that's arrogance (Proverbs 8:13). Instead of being interested in others, you're only interested in exalting yourself. Arrogance is a people repellent. The most arrogant people are the most lonely and joyless because all they want to do is talk, but no one wants to listen.

The good news is there are solutions to our pride. First, get in the habit of asking for help, and don't reject help when it's offered. Instead of figuring out how to do things on your own, invite others in to help. You will likely get it down faster and better. Or, it may be less efficient, or you could have done it better by yourself. But what you gain is an experience with a friend and investment in the relationship. So often, we don't want to appear weak to others, but weakness brings us together.

Second, ask others for advice. Proverbs 15:22-23 says, "Without counsel plans fail, but with many advisers they succeed. To make an apt answer is a *joy* to a man, and a word in season, how good it is!" Bringing people into your decision-making and receiving sound counsel will give you joy! Why? Because you will be humbled, and they will feel honored. And you can celebrate with them when things go well and have them to fall back on if they don't.

Third, eagerly serve others. Actively and consistently find a place to serve in your church. Don't be flaky; be faithful. Also, a great principle to live by in everyday life is to be first to serve and last to be served. When there are times to be served, go last. Let others go before you in the food line. Get in the practice of putting others before yourself. Also, be first to serve when you are asked and serve even when you're not. Do the tasks that no one else wants to do. "Trash needs to be taken out? I'm on it!" When you do this, you will discover incredible inner joy when your mindset shifts from I *have* to serve to I *get* to serve.

Fourth, genuinely take an interest in others (Philippians 2:4). Instead of talking about yourself, ask people questions and be a great listener. Ask them about their lives, jobs, upbrings, families, interests, and hobbies. You'll learn that people are really interesting! You should go into a conversation not looking to tell people about you, but you learn something new about them. The end goal for every conversation shouldn't be for people to walk away thinking how great you are but walk away thinking how great Jesus is and how loved they are. If you do this, they will feel seen, known, and loved because you genuinely took an interest in them. That creates a deeper connection, producing joy in them and you.

REFLECTION AND DISCUSSION QUESTIONS

1. Do you have a habit of being on your phone around people? What steps can you take to change that?
2. What thoughts from your Critic do you deal with the most? How has your Critic made you feel disconnected from others?

3. In what ways do you compare yourself to others?
4. What do you complain about the most? What steps can you take to help you not complain anymore?
5. Is there anyone that you need to forgive? Is there anyone that you need to ask forgiveness?
6. In what ways have you been wearing a mask? Is there any hidden sin that you need to confess to others?
7. Of the different ways we can be prideful, which one do you struggle with the most? How are you going to pursue humility intentionally?

CHAPTER EIGHT

Complete Joy

When I was in 6th grade, I was bullied profusely at church. Remember the kid drawing monkeys shooting cannonballs? Yeah, well, just a month after putting my faith in Jesus, I went on a youth group retreat. Now, I got picked on at youth group pretty regularly. Kids would call me names and exclude me from games (call me Rudolph). But the retreat was the worst of all.

We went to a campsite in the middle of nowhere in Yorkville, Illinois (I lived in the Chicago suburbs then). All the kids stayed in cabins, and I was assigned a room with almost all 8th graders, and we had no adult supervision. Looking back now, that youth pastor should have gotten fired! As you can imagine, that scenario was just asking for trouble, and it was for me. I was constantly called names that I can't write in this book. I was shoved into bedposts. I couldn't sleep at night because they constantly kicked my bed (top bunk), threw shoes at me, and stole my sleeping bag. It was a living nightmare for five days. But the worst came the last night.

When I came back into the cabin after the evening worship session, I noticed all my clothes were missing from my bag. I looked all over the cabin but couldn't find them. Did they put them in someone else's bag? Or take them to another cabin? Or throw them outside? My search ended when I went to the bathroom, and there I found my clothes on the ground, where they had been peed on. Yeah, brutal.

I went home the next day and didn't tell anyone what happened. I was so angry and ashamed. I left that campsite angry at those kids, angry at church, and angry at God. Remember, I was a baby believer who had just given my life to Jesus. From that moment, I decided I didn't want anything to do with church. I would go on Sundays because I had to, but I didn't go to youth group or desire to have any "church friends." Frankly, I hated church because it reminded me of how I had been hurt.

Five years later, I was in a dark place. I didn't really have faith and was borderline atheist. I made bad choices that isolated me from my family and friends. I was so lost, and one day, I did something I hadn't done in years. *Pray.* I remember it being so simple. All I could say was, "Lord, I need you" over and over again. At that moment, I felt the Lord's warm, gracious presence. I realized He had never left me, even if I had left Him. I confessed and asked for forgiveness for what I had done and asked for His help to walk with Him, really for the first time.

The next day at school, two girls I knew came to my locker and said, "Hey, you should come to our youth group tonight!" *Youth group?* That's where I got bullied. I hated youth group. But I also just had this encounter with the Lord, and this was a different church. What do I do? I took a leap of faith and went that night. I needed Jesus and friends, and well, let's be honest, two girls asked me.

That invitation changed my life forever. I was absorbed into a beautiful church community that loved me, discipled me, and helped me grow in my faith. I established deep friendships with people who were passionately pursuing Jesus. I was even eventually given leadership opportunities to serve and lead a group. That's where I first felt a call to ministry. That time shaped my Christian life in college as an adult and shaped the way I do ministry. As I reflect, I think about that broken and hurt kid calling out for Jesus to help. I told Jesus I needed Him, and He sent me His people. He gave me what I needed, and that was church community.

Complete Joy is Found in Community

In order to abide in Jesus, we must be connected to His church. We cannot flourish in our faith without the fellowship of other believers. Think back to the vines and branches. Notice a small detail in John 15:5. Jesus said, "I am the vine, and you are the *branches*." Notice that branches are not singular; they are plural. So often, we read Scripture only thinking about ourselves. But this vine doesn't just have one branch, but many. Our lives need to be intertwined with other branches connected to the vine. We have joy when we are deeply connected to Jesus *and others*.

That's why the apostles say that joy is complete in fellowship. Paul, addressing believers he knew, said in Philippians 2:2, "*Complete my joy* by being of the same mind, having the same love, being in full accord and of one mind." John, addressing believers he didn't know yet, said in 1 John 1:4, "We are writing these things so that our *joy may be complete*." In agreement with Jesus and the rest of Scripture, the apostles are saying that joy is experienced to its fullest when we are friends with other believers. As I shared in the previous chapter, joy is incomplete in isolation but complete in the community.

But you don't accidentally become deeply connected in church community; you do it intentionally. Standing in a gym doesn't make you fit; you have to show up and do the work. Likewise, you can't just show up to church, sit in a chair, and expect to have deep relationships. We have to put in the work. But studies show that even showing up to church is a struggle for Christians.

In 2024, Gallup released a survey with results concerning church attendance. Surveying professing Protestant Christians showed that 30% attend every week, 14% attend almost every week, 13% attend once a month, 27% attend seldom, and 16% never attend church.[88] That means roughly 44% are consistently in church, while 56% of professing Christians are never at church or 12 times a year at best. It is no wonder why Christians are struggling to have joy because most Christians are disconnected from the local church.

But, let's be honest, church attendance is only part of the issue. As I shared in the previous chapter, you can be an every-week attender and still be very disconnected and lonely. Being involved in a church community and having deep friendships takes a big investment. A Kansas University Study showed how much time is needed to make friends:

50+ Hours Casual Friend (superficial conversations and lack emotional connection)

90+ Hours Friend (meaningful conversations and know each other's likes and interests)

200+ Hours Close Friend (deep connection and conversations and know each other's secrets and struggles) [89]

What's important to note is that friendships are formed not just by the quantity of time spent but also by the quality of time spent. For example, the study found that environments like school and work, where people spend the most time with others, produced fewer close friendships. Again, proximity doesn't equal intimacy. Instead, it was outside of these environments where people grew deeper friendships. When they hang out at people's houses, eat food, play games, and so on.[90] The bottom line is that it takes extra time and effort to form friendships. Friendships take a lot of work, but it's worth it. The researcher, Jeffery Hall, said, "We have to put that time in…You can't snap your fingers and make a friend. Maintaining close relationships is the most important work we do in our lives — most people on their deathbeds agree."[91]

So, can you form deep relationships with others by just attending church? Honestly, I don't see how that's possible. Think about it like this: let's say you're an every-week church attender. On any given Sunday, most of the time, you're standing and sitting in a row for an hour to an hour and a half. There might be a greet time, which is 2-ish minutes. Maybe you talk to people before and after service, so we'll say, at best, you get 15-ish minutes. So, let's just call it an even 20-ish minutes of interaction. Doing the math, if all you did was attend church, it would take you 11.5 years to have close friends. If you were a twice-a-month attender, it would take 23 years, and once a month, 50 years. Now, that's also assuming that the 20 minutes of conversations you have on a Sunday are deep and meaningful, which likely it's not. The point is that even a consistent church attendance is not enough. To form meaningful relationships, it takes time and effort outside of the church as well.

This is what made the early church so deeply connected. Act 2:46 says, "And day by day, attending the temple together and breaking bread in their homes, they received their food with glad and generous hearts." Did you catch that? Not just Sunday, but *day by day*. They saw each other nearly every day. Hebrews 10:24-25 says, "And let us consider how we may spur one another on toward love and good deeds, *not giving up meeting together,* as some are in the habit of doing, but encouraging one another—and all the more as you see the Day approaching." Boy, is that a verse for this generation!

Our problem is that we have our priorities backward. We try to work church community into our schedules, but instead, we should work our schedules around church community. Church shouldn't be the thing getting cut. Our relationships with other believers have to be our highest priority. So, make Sunday service a priority. Make greeting others and introducing yourself to people you don't know a priority. Make inviting people over for dinner a priority. Make Bible study with others a priority. Make eating lunch with a potential friend a priority. Make serving somewhere in your church a priority. Even make inviting people to do fun things a priority. You can't make people be your friends, but you sure can invite them to be. Community is not found; it is formed.

Having fun and eating food are important for making friends, but Jesus calls us to something even deeper. He calls us to *love one another*. Jesus said in John 13:34-35 "A new commandment I give to you, that you love one another: just as I have loved you, you also are to love one another. By this all people will know that you are my disciples, if you have love for one another." Notice He says that we are to love another the way He loves us. And when you love others in that way, people will take notice. Love would mark us because love is also a fruit of the Spirit. We don't skip love to get to joy; it's through love that we have joy! So, how do we love in this way? In order to love the way Jesus loves us we must be unconditionally and sacrificially committed to one another. What does that look like? Let's explore that next.

OUR TRIBE

Having lots of friends is a treasure in life, but what we really need is close family and friends—people with whom we spend the most time, who are our first call when we need help, with whom we are safe to share our struggles, who are passionately pursuing Jesus along with us, and who are devoted to one another. How I see it, we all need a *tribe*.

In Scripture, tribes were typically families descending from a common ancestor. For example, the twelve tribes of Israel were the descendants of Abraham and his sons. Today, you see tribes in different countries and cultures. And yes, even Survivor has tribes. But for us, our tribe is our spiritual family, consisting of our actual family and other believers. All believers are a part of the kingdom and God's family. Still, our tribe is a specific group of people who are intentionally pursuing Jesus together and committed to loving one another.

Naturally, a major part of our tribe is our family. They are our number one priority to love. If we love others but don't love our family well, we've missed the mark entirely. But in addition to our family, we all need some kind of small group. Your church may call them life groups, connect groups, or home groups. These people we meet with consistently and intentionally do life with and are real with. If you're not in a home group, I highly encourage you to be. Whether you join a group or start one, groups are vital to our spiritual growth. Rows are good, but circles are better.

Taking several of the "one another" verses from Scripture, I created TRIBES, an acronym that is the DNA of how we are to love one another. TRIBES can be implemented in our families, groups, and relationships. If you don't feel close to the people in your life, TRIBES is a guide that will help you go deeper. If our tribe commits to loving one another using TRIBES, we will experience the complete joy we are created for.

Tell One Another the Truth
Rejoice With One Another
Intercede For One Another
Bear One Another's Burdens
Encourage One Another
Serve One Another

Tell One Another The Truth

Can you see your face? Like, right now, try looking at your face. You can't, right? I think of the SpongeBob episode when SpongeBob asked Patrick why he was mad. Patrick replies,

"Cause I can't see my forehead." I feel that Patrick, I really do. If you have no idea what I'm talking about, you should look it up on YouTube. It'll be worth it.

So how can you see your face? Typically, you look in a mirror. You do this every single day when you wake up in the morning (hopefully), when you brush your teeth (really hope so), and after you go to the bathroom and wash your hands (really, really hope so). A mirror helps you see what you otherwise can't on your own. Our face is a "blind spot." But our face is not the only blind spots in our lives. We have many blind spots in our walk with Jesus. One way we can see our blind spots is through God's Word, which is like a mirror (James 1:22-23).

We all need a tribe devoted to God's Word, the Word of truth. Each person is devoted to looking in the biblical mirror every day, just like they look in their physical mirror every day. They look in the mirror not to see how good they are but how good Jesus is and how badly we need Him. The tribe is constantly looking to be transformed by the Word of Truth. We even have the Spirit of Truth who indwells us and will guide the tribe in all truth (John 16:13).

Then, because our tribe is devoted to the Word of Truth and indwelled by the Spirit of Truth, we can speak truth into one another's lives. Ephesians 4:15 says, "Speaking the *truth in love*, we are to grow up in every way into him who is the head, into Christ." Just like the Word, our tribe can address blind spots in each other's lives that we otherwise can't see. For example, "Hey, I think you need to be more careful with your tone and how you say things," or "I'm not sure if you should be watching that show," or "I think you may be seeking the approval of people by doing that."

Speaking the truth is never to condemn or to bring shame. It's always motivated by love. Our tribe should love one another too much to let each other walk or fall into sin. Sometimes, the conversation will be awkward and challenging, but it will bring your tribe closer together. We live in a day where any of us can be swept away from the truth and start believing and living in lies (Ephesians 4:14). And if Satan's primary weapon is lies, then our greatest counter-weapon is the truth and our tribe.

In addition to speaking the truth, our tribe must be devoted to telling one another the truth. This means being completely transparent about everything in our lives. There are no lies or secrets. As I shared in the previous chapter, our love must be sincere, meaning our tribe is committed to not wearing any masks (Romans 12:9). If we want to be transformed, we have to be transparent.

Jonathan Pokluda, pastor of Harris Creek Baptist Church, champions transparency at the church he pastors. They do something I believe would be very helpful for you and your tribe. Each person answers three questions in their life groups (small groups/home groups). Each person shares, and then someone in the tribe prays for them. They continue until everyone shares and is prayed for. Here are the three questions:

- **Input** – How did you feed your soul? How is your Bible reading and prayer life?
- **Output** – How did you feed others? Did you serve, disciple, or share the gospel with anyone during the week?
- **Confession** – How did you feed your flesh? What sins do you need to confess to others?[92]

I encourage you in your tribe to answer these questions and commit to telling the truth. Then, you can be fully loved, free, and known. Your tribe is a mask-free zone.

This may be uncomfortable at first. But since your tribe is devoted to the Word of Truth, has the Spirit of Truth, speaks the truth in love, and tells one another the truth, the truth will build *trust*. And it is a treasure to have people you can trust with your life. And with that, your tribe can rejoice because "Love *rejoices* with the truth." (1 Corinthians 13:6)

Rejoice With One Another

Celebration is not just a catchy song from the 80's that everybody sings and dances to when it's played (just me?). Celebration is a biblical practice for the church, especially in our tribe. Paul says in Romans 12:15, "*Rejoice* with those who *rejoice*," and in 1 Corinthians 12:26, "If one member is honored, all *rejoice* together." When we rejoice with those who rejoice, we have genuine joy for what God is doing in someone else's life. The good that happens in other lives is our good as well. Their joy is our joy!

The early church was used to celebrating because it was rooted in Scripture and Jewish culture. God institutes a rhythm of celebrating for His people, starting with Passover (Exodus 12). Then, six other festivals and feasts were added to create a calendar of celebrations (Leviticus 23). But even beyond the calendared holidays, the people celebrated special occasions. For example, when Solomon built the Temple in Jerusalem, the people had a dedication celebration for seven days full of eating, singing, and dancing, and they "went to their homes *joyful* and glad of heart for all the goodness that the Lord had shown to David, his servant and to Israel his people" (1 Kings 8:66). God's people knew how to party!

God even gave His people instructions on how to celebrate. In Deuteronomy 14:26, God told his people to "spend the money for whatever you desire—oxen or sheep or wine or strong drink, whatever your appetite craves. And you shall eat there before the Lord your God and *rejoice*, you and your household." Did you catch that? God instructed His people to spend money on things they enjoy, more specifically whatever they craved, and drink and eat great food with each other. Now, God didn't permit self-indulgence and sin. Notice *who* they are celebrating. *God.* They were to eat, enjoy, and rejoice in the Lord. Joyful celebrations are not self-centered; they are God-centered. We celebrate by giving God the credit for what He's done and is doing for us, through us, and to us.

In his book, *The Spirit of the Disciplines*, Dallas Willard wrote that celebrating is a spiritual discipline and an act of worship. He wrote:

> It is the completion of worship, for it dwells on the greatness of God as shown in his goodness *to us*. We engage in celebration when we enjoy ourselves, our life, our world, *in conjunction with our faith* and confidence in God's greatness, beauty, and goodness. We concentrate on *our* life and world as God's work and as God's gift to us…we come together with others who know God to eat and drink, to sing and dance, and to relate stories of God's action for our lives and our people.[93]

Celebrating is a holy act of worship. Of course, "partying" has a negative connotation because the enemy tries to ruin what is supposed to be godly. But, as followers of Jesus, we ought to be the best partyers because we party with a purpose!

We should celebrate our annual holidays for our faith and country (Christmas, Easter, Fourth of July, etc.). Some of these holidays already should be focused on Jesus. But, even on the holidays that aren't, add Jesus in! Get your tribe together, get the crockpot out and grill out, worship together, play games, and talk about how good God is.

Also, we should celebrate birthdays and anniversaries well. Do whatever you enjoy and what's meaningful to you on that day and give God the glory. I'll share something impactful about how our family celebrates birthdays. Something our youth ministry does is called "birthday blessings." When it's someone's birthday, we go around and tell the person about the growth we've seen in the last year, what makes them awesome, and tell them how much they are loved. We've implemented birthday blessings into our families and tribe, and that is easily the highlight. The gifts, food, and fellowship are always good, but birthday blessings are the best gift of all.

Also, we should celebrate special occasions well. For example, graduation, new jobs, promotions, moving to a new house, reaching a financial goal like paying off a loan, or becoming debt-free. Any milestone or achievement needs to be celebrated with our tribe. Even small achievements like getting an A on a test, getting your first hit in T-ball, or finishing a home improvement project. However big the achievement should determine how big the celebration is. Whether we get steaks at Longhorn or slushies at Sonic, we rejoice when we share our achievements with our tribe, giving the Lord glory for what He's done.

Also, we need to celebrate spiritual markers and growth especially. Whether it's being baptized, leading someone to Christ, or celebrating God by answering a prayer, we must celebrate with our church family, especially with our tribe. Some of our friends celebrate their spiritual birthdays every year when they give their lives to Jesus. They get their tribe together, eat, worship, and encourage one another. I love that! Again, the purpose of celebrating is to rejoice in the Lord with others. When we do, we join in with the celebration that is going on in heaven (Luke 15:10)!

So, whatever the occasion is, let's celebrate!

Intercede For One Another

Do you have a praying grandma? I do. Grandma Karen is the biggest prayer warrior I know. Every day, she prays for her children, grandchildren, great-grandchildren, and friends, all by name and with specific requests. I can confidently say that I am a product of her faithful prayers. Most people are unaware she prays for them, but the power is evident.

What Grandma Karen does and what many faithful saints do is called intercessory prayer.

To *intercede* means to go forth on someone else's behalf. Jesus and the Spirit are described as intercessors for us. In Hebrews 7:25, the writer says Jesus "always lives to make *intercession* for them [the church]." In Romans 8:26, Paul says, "Likewise, the Spirit helps us in our weakness. For we do not know what to pray for as we ought, but the Spirit himself *intercedes* for us with groanings too deep for words." Think about that: even when you don't know what to pray, Jesus and the Spirit are praying for you on your behalf. How cool is that? But just like Jesus and the Spirit intercede, we are called to intercede for others. Paul says in 1 Timothy 2:1, "I urge that supplications, prayers, *intercessions*, and thanksgivings be made for all people." We are called to intercede for all people, but especially our tribe.

When Paul wrote his letter to the church in Ephesus, we closed the letter talking about the enemy we fight but do not see. Famously, he instructed the church to put on the spiritual full armor of God, which is the belt of truth, the breastplate of righteousness, shoes of readiness of the gospel, the shield of faith, the helmet of salvation, the sword of the Spirit, which is the Word of God (Ephesians 6:13-17). I'm not sure if you've noticed this, but do you know what part the spiritual armor leaves us exposed? Our *back*.

When we read Scripture, we often read it in an individualistic way. But Paul was not writing to an individual; he was writing to a church. In other words, he wasn't writing to a soldier; he was writing to an *army*. We can't go into battle against evil on our own and expect to win. The enemy fights dirty and will exploit our weaknesses and vulnerabilities any chance they get. We need our tribe, who will cover each other's backs every day. And we cover each other's backs by interceding for one another. Paul concludes the armor of God passage by saying, "praying at all times in the Spirit, with all prayer and supplication. To that end, keep alert with all perseverance, making supplication for all the saints" (Ephesians 6:18).

When we pray, we change the battlefield. It's like how an eagle fights a snake. An eagle will not fight a snake on the ground, where the snake is powerful and deadly. Rather, the eagle picks the snake up where it has no stamina, power, or balance. The snake is useless, weak, and vulnerable in the air. Then, the eagle will drop the snake from the sky, killing it and enjoying a nice meal. When the eagle changes the battleground, it has a sure victory.

When we fight the enemy, we can't fight him on his turf. So often, we try to fight him in our flesh and willpower, but we fail. We must change the battleground, which is what we do when we pray. When we fight with prayer, we fight in the spiritual realm, and God takes over our battle. When we intercede, the enemy is defenseless and weak, like a snake in the sky.

That said, we need to know what we need to pray for. What needs does our tribe have? Also, what are each other's most vulnerable places? We need to know these things so we can specifically pray for provision and protection. We need to commit to pray for each other in person when we are together but also when we are apart. Having a prayer notebook or cards is helpful because we can flip through them daily and know exactly what to pray for. Even setting an alarm on your phone daily to stop and pray for your tribe is also a good practice. We should do whatever it takes to help us intentionally intercede for one another. And as our tribe intercedes, we pray with joy because we know we have each other's backs. Echoing Paul in Philippians 1:4-5, "In all my prayers for all of you, I always pray with *joy* because of your partnership in the gospel from the first day until now."

Bear One Another's Burdens

Last Fall, we were hanging out at my parents' house one Sunday evening. While cleaning the dishes after dinner, I got a weather alert on my phone that a severe storm was approaching. Fifteen minutes later, I heard a pop. Then another pop. Then these pops turned into bangs, as if someone was hitting the house with baseball bats. But it wasn't baseball bats; they were hailstorms the size of baseballs. It hailed ice baseballs for twenty straight minutes. Yeah. After the storm was over, we assessed the damage. All our cars, including Samantha's, my parents, and mine, were completely totaled (4 cars, Sam's being brand new). In addition to the cars, my parent's house had excessive roof damage and broken siding and windows. Between the cars and house, there was over $130,000 in damage. Thank God for insurance.

But insurance wasn't going to clean up the damage, get us to work, or take us to doctor appointments. We thought, *"What are we going to do?"* Well, that's what a tribe is for. The day after the storm, my sister and brother-in-law took off work and took the kids out of school to help clean up debris. What would have taken us weeks to clean up took us only a day. We had two friends drive Samantha and me to doctor appointments. A church member lent me his F-150 to drive (soooo much fun). Our senior adults pastor lent us his car for a whole month! And so many others helped us when we needed it the most. That is what a tribe does.

Paul says in Galatians 6:2, "Bear one another's burdens, and so fulfill the law of Christ."

To bear burdens means to carry heavy weight. You know exactly what this means if you have ever moved or helped someone move. It's impossible to carry heavy furniture on your own. So, we ask family and friends to help us or hire a moving company. The point is that we can't carry the weight on our own. We need others to help us carry it. And that is the picture Paul painted for us. Some things in life are heavy, and we can't carry them on our own. We need other's help to carry the weight. We need a tribe.

Our tribe should be first responders to bear one another's burdens. That's what the first-century church did. When there was a physical or material need, the church shared its time and resources to help (Acts 2:45). Our tribe should do the same. If there's a financial burden, like an unexpected medical expense, we should be more than willing to help collectively. Or, if someone is sick or recovering from surgery, we should find ways to be helpful. Create a meal train, cut the grass, or clean the house. So often, we don't want to be a burden to others, so we don't ask for help, and we try to do everything alone. But as we explored in the previous chapter, pride is a joy thief. Ask for help, and don't deny help if you are asked.

Although many burdens are physical and material, they can also affect us emotionally. In Romans 12:15, Paul said, "Rejoice with those who rejoice, *weep* with those who *weep*." In our tribe, when one suffers, we all suffer; when one hurts, we all hurt. This is especially true when we grieve.

The best thing we can do to bear one another's grieving burdens is to be helpful and be present. After Job lost his health, his house, his business, and his children, his three friends "sat with him on the ground seven days and seven nights, and no one spoke a word to him, for they saw that his suffering was very great." (Job 2:13) Everything was fine until Job's friends opened their mouths. In grieving times, we don't need to preach; we just need to be present. Just sit with them in silence, listen if they want to talk, and cry together. Then, in time, as the Psalmist says, "Those who sow in tears shall reap with shouts of *joy*!"(Psalm 126:5) We'll explore joy in suffering more in the next chapter.

Encourage One Another

When I was younger, I was really into Legos. Okay, let's be honest: I'm still really into Legos. But as a child, I enjoyed building large Lego sets, often thousands of pieces, and took a long time to build. As much as I enjoyed building Lego sets, my younger brother, Grant, equally enjoyed destroying them. It would infuriate me. But, when Grant became old enough, we built together instead of destroying my Lego sets, which gave me a lot of joy. Likewise, we need a tribe committed to building each other up instead of tearing each other down.

Paul says, "Therefore encourage one another and build one another up, just as you are doing" (1 Thessalonians 5:11). Paul would know this firsthand because he experienced this encouragement in his own life. Most people don't know this, but Paul was discipled by Barnabas, whose nickname means "Son of Encouragement." Barnabas is a minor person in the book of Acts, but his ministry had an incredible impact on the church. When Paul was converted, the apostles feared him and sent Barnabas to meet with him and check him out (Acts 9:27). Barnabas was the one who vouched for Paul and said he was a brother. Can you imagine if Barnabas said no? But Barnabas didn't focus on what Paul had done. He saw the genuineness of his faith and saw what he could *become*. That's what an encourager does.

Then, for several years, Barnabas discipled Paul in ministry, teaching and preaching. As the book of Acts progresses, Paul steps into the lead role while Barnabas recedes into the background. But that's what an encourager does. They stay in the background, cheering others on and watching them grow, which gives them great joy. John Ortberg comments on Barnabas: "His joy was in recognizing and developing greatness in somebody else. Paul's ministry went on to be far more visible than his own, and nobody rejoiced more than Barnabas did."[94]

Like Barnabas, we should strive to be encouragers that build others up in our tribe. We should intentionally look for the potential in others and tell them where we see gifting and growth. Often, encouragement is seeing something special in someone else that they don't see in themselves. Encouragement, in its simplest form, is to give someone else *courage*. Fear holds us back a lot in life. But when we encourage one another, we light a fire of courage where there was once fear, and our role is to keep that fire going. We do that by telling another, "I see this in you," or "You are so gifted," or "You're doing a great job; keep it up!" And the tribe rejoices when we see growth and success. Encouragement inspires us to get started, but it also inspires us to keep going.

In our tribe, we have friends who run marathons, ultra marathons, and triathlons. Apparently, a marathon wasn't long enough, so they made some "ultra." Yes, for fun. I'm incredibly impressed by them! Because of their interest, I've become interested too. Not that I'm going to run a marathon (I'm not there yet), but I'm interested in the sport. Here's a question: when do most people quit a marathon? For clarity, a marathon is 26.2 miles long. Most people quit on average at mile marker 20, just six miles from the finish.[95] Isn't that crazy? This is when runners typically hit the "marathon wall," where they are physically and mentally exhausted and unaware of how long they have to go. So they quit just shy of the finish line. But, what helps runners push through the marathon wall is to have family and friends along the way to cheer them on and to let them know they are almost there. Likewise, this is a picture of what a tribe does.

Life has challenges, and circumstances can be discouraging. Failures and mistakes are a given in life. Even the tests and trials of our faith are difficult to overcome. Naturally, there are times we just want to tap out and quit. But, as a tribe, we are supposed to be each other's biggest cheerleaders, cheering on each other in these challenges. To let one another know, "You can do it!" and "Don't give up!" "You're not alone. We're right here with you!" Even when we stumble and fall, our tribe is there to pick us back up. Encouragement gives us the endurance to finish strong. And when we do, we rejoice!

Serve One Another

When I was ordained, my senior pastor presented me with a bowl and towel. He told me that as pastors, we are called to be shepherds, counselors, teachers, and preachers, but our most important job was to be chief feet washers. We are to take the lowly position of a servant and live a life of service. I have that bowl in my office, and I see it every day. It's a physical reminder for me, right next to my prosthetic leg (a reference to chapter six).

Being a feet washer isn't just for pastors; it's for every follower of Jesus. The night of the last supper, Jesus got a bowl and towel, and one by one, He washed His disciple's feet. Remember, these guys weren't wearing Nike or Brooks. They wore open sandals where dirt and animal feces from the streets made their feet filthy. But Jesus served each of them by washing their feet. Peter was a bit resistant, but Jesus straightened him out pretty quickly. And then Jesus said this in John 13:14-15, "If I then, your Lord and Teacher, have washed your feet, you also ought to wash one another's feet. For I have given you an example, that you also should do just as I have done to you." Jesus washed His disciple's feet to give them an example to follow. It was an example for them but also an example for us, especially our tribe.

Paul says in Galatians 5:13, "For you were called to freedom, brothers. Only do not use your freedom as an opportunity for the flesh, but through *love serve one another.*" We aren't to use our freedom to serve ourselves but others. We are not looking to be served but to serve. And Jesus was the example. Even though He was the Lord of the universe, He humbled Himself to the position of a servant (Philippians 2:6-7). None of us are above anyone. We're also not above any task. Feet washing was a dirty job. We all should be willing to take on the dirty jobs of serving one another. And our motivation should not be to get something in return, like a reward or recognition. Rather, our motivation should purely be *love*. Our tribe ought to have the mindset of a foot washer, which, as Paul says, produces complete joy (Philippians 2:2).

Also, as we serve one another, we should serve *with* one another. Something supernaturally powerful happens when we serve together. You've probably experienced this on a mission trip or some kind of service project. The Spirit bonds us when we work together to love our neighbors. Hanging out and eating together is great but serving with one another may be the most bonding thing you can do as a tribe. We bond because we are fulfilling our purpose of being the body of Christ. Ephesians 4:16 says, "From whom the whole body, joined and held together by every joint with which it is equipped when each part is working properly, makes the body grow so that it builds itself up in *love*." When we serve together, we not only fulfill God's purpose but also find true joy in community.

I encourage you to find ways for your tribe to serve together. For example, look up your soup kitchens and local food pantries and see how you can get involved. See if a local elementary school has a book-reading club for struggling kids. Ask your church staff if any widows need help with yard work or chores. The possibilities are endless in the ways you can serve together. Work together, commit to it, and watch your joy become complete.

REFLECTION AND DISCUSSION QUESTIONS

1. How many close friends do you have?
2. Do you prioritize investing in friendship with other believers? How so? In what ways can you improve?
3. What's a time you felt complete joy spending time with others? What made it so joyful for you?
4. Of the different components of TRIBES, what do you find is the most difficult to do? Why?

5. Of the different components of TRIBES, what do you feel you need the most right now? Why?
6. How can you intentionally implement TRIBES in your families, small group, and friends?

CHAPTER NINE

Joy in Suffering

A couple of years ago, we were hustling and bustling through a busy summer. With Samantha and I both being on staff at our church, almost every week, we had some kind of event. Samantha had VBS, Kids Camp, and Preteen Camp, and I had just launched our young adults Bible Study on Thursday nights. It was exciting and exhausting, and we were especially excited and exhausted because, secretly, we were expecting our second child. Samantha was pregnant, and we were over the moon.

Right before Preteen Camp, we went in for our routine 12-week appointment. Samantha was right on track, and the baby was healthy and growing. We sat in the waiting room extra-long that day. We finally got called back to do an ultrasound room to check on the baby. After several moments, I noticed the ultrasound technician's cheery demeanor become solemn. I'll never forget what she said next, "I'm sorry, I don't see a heartbeat today." We learned that our baby had passed away a week before. Our hearts were shattered.

What would follow is months of grief, fear, anger, and overwhelming sadness. I wrote in my journal weeks after finding out, *"My heart is frantic. I want to cry, yell, run, punch, and sleep all at the same time."* Sam said to me one day on the couch, *"I don't know if I'll ever have joy again."*

I share this with you because Samantha and I felt strongly from the Lord to do so. We know many of you have or are experiencing loss. You may have a similar story to ours. Or perhaps you have lost a loved one. Or maybe you've lost your job. Or maybe you've lost good health. Or maybe you've lost your marriage. Whatever you've gone through, going through, or will go through, we want to let you know there is hope. And yes, you can even have joy in your suffering and sorrow.

I purposely put this chapter at the end of the book because everything we've learned to this point enables us to have joy in suffering. You can't have joy in suffering without abiding in Jesus, nor can you if you are disconnected from people. By staying deeply connected to Jesus and others, we can have joy in our suffering. It's believed that Jesus taught the parable of the vines and branches to His disciples because they were about to endure much suffering. They were going to be brutally persecuted and lose family, friends, and eventually their own lives. But even though they endured those sufferings, all of them wrote about how joyful they were. How? Because they abided in the true vine. They stayed intertwined with their tribe and loved one another.

Of all the apostles, Paul wrote the most about joy and suffering. Though he wasn't present when Jesus taught the vine and branches (he was made an apostle later), His dependence on Christ and connection to others was evident, and because of that, he had great joy.

Paul endured much suffering in his life, so he can speak from his own experience. In 2 Corinthians 11:23-29, he shares his resume of suffering. He was whipped with 39 lashes five times, beaten with rods three times, stoned one time, and arrested and imprisoned too many times to count. He endured dangerous journeys at risk for his life, involving being shipwrecked three times and stranded adrift once, countless sleepless nights, starvation and dehydration, and freezing conditions. He was even bitten by a venous snake once but didn't die (Acts 28:3). Imagine using that as a conversation starter. Yet, he says, "In all our affliction, I am overflowing with *joy*." (2 Corinthians 7:4). Wait, did we miss something? How is it possible to have joy in suffering?

This is a paradox that just doesn't seem possible. But for Christians, it is possible. Paul even tells us the reason Christians can have joy in suffering in Romans 5:3-5. Paul says, "We *rejoice* in our sufferings, knowing that suffering produces endurance, and endurance produces character, and character produces hope, and hope does not put us to shame, because God's love has been poured into our hearts through the Holy Spirit who has been given to us" (NIV).

Notice that Paul doesn't tell us how, but he tells us *why*. He says we rejoice in our suffering *"knowing that"* (NIV), or some translations say, *"because we know that"* (CSB). This type of knowledge is a belief based on facts. For example, we don't have to be afraid to jump because of the fear of floating off into space. Rather, we can jump as high as we want *because we know that* gravity will bring us back down. Likewise, Paul is saying we can rejoice in our suffering *because we know that* God uses our suffering for a purpose. He doesn't give us a self-help three-step process to follow to have joy in suffering, but he does give three reasons why we should have joy in our suffering. Let's unpack each one together.

SUFFERING MAKES US STRONGER

For the last thirty years, the University of Arizona has been conducting research experiments in Biosphere Two, a giant greenhouse facility in the middle of the desert. The goal of their research is to see if the Earth's ecosystem could survive on a space station or another planet. Isn't that crazy? It sounds like something from a movie. But Biosphere Two is real, and scientists are still doing experiments today.

In the 1990s, when Biosphere Two was just getting started, the researchers experimented with growing trees. The bubble had perfect soil, rain, and sun conditions. As they observed, they noticed their trees were growing faster than they would in nature. They were excited for what seemed to be a major success. But, right before reaching full maturity, the trees fell over—literally. The scientists were shocked and left scratching their heads. Why did these near-perfect trees fall over? After examining the tree's root system and consulting experts, they determined the issue was the lack of *wind*.

Scientists learned that in nature, trees have what are called "stress roots." When a tree grows, wind and storms constantly impact it, and in response to the wind, the tree is stimulated to grow more roots to go deep and wide so it can stand strong. But without wind or storms, stress roots are not grown, and the tree is left with a weak root system that won't be able to sustain its body or growth and will eventually fall over. Trees don't grow well in a bubble.

Biosphere Two is an example of what we try to do in our own lives today. We want to create controlled environments (a bubble) where our lives are comfortable and have little stress or suffering. We won't take risks where there is a potential of something being hard or us getting hurt. I'm not talking about jumping out of an airplane, but risks like sharing the gospel with your neighbor, sacrificially giving more to your church, or starting a hard conversation with a friend. Naturally, if we're given the choice between difficult and easy, we will choose the easiest almost every time. But living in a bubble doesn't strengthen your faith; it weakens it.

As much as we try to control and avoid suffering, there is a lot of suffering we can't control or avoid. Car accidents happen. Cancer diagnoses happen. Children make really bad choices happen. These are just some of the storms that come our way, and as much as we want to control them, we can't.

Naturally, we hate suffering in all its kinds. But suffering is actually good for us. Not suffering in of itself, but what suffering *produces*. Like trees, storms in life stimulate us to grow faith roots deep and wide so that we become stronger. As Colossians 2:6-7 says, "Therefore, as you received Christ Jesus the Lord, so walk in him, *rooted* and *built up* in him and *established* in the faith, just as you were taught, abounding in thanksgiving." When suffering happens, that means God is doing something, and we can find joy in that.

Paul says, "We *rejoice* in our sufferings, knowing that suffering *produces endurance*" (Romans 5:3). What's interesting is that the word Paul uses for endurance is the same word James uses in his joy-in-suffering verses, but it's translated "steadfastness." James 1:2-4 says, "Count it all *joy*, my brothers, when you meet trials of various kinds, for you know that the testing of your faith produces *steadfastness*. And let steadfastness have its full effect, that you may be perfect and complete, lacking in nothing."

The Greek word Paul and James use is *hypomeno*, which, broken down, is *hypo*, meaning "under," and *meno*, which is our word for "to abide" or "remain or dwell." Ah, we find abiding and joy together again! This kind of abiding is remaining even under immense pressure. This is the same word Jesus used in Matthew 10:22 "And you will be hated by all for my name's sake. But the one who endures (hypomeno) to the end will be saved." The author of Hebrews said about Jesus in Hebrew 12:2, "looking to Jesus, the founder and perfecter of our faith, who for the *joy* that was set before him endured (hypomeno) the cross, despising the shame, and is seated at the right hand of the throne of God." Suffering is the only way to produce strong abiding, a stronger connection with the Vine. For lack of better words, suffering produces a "never giving up" faith—a steadfast, enduring, and resilient faith in Jesus.

In these joy-in-suffering passages, the authors often use *trials* to refer to suffering times. We just read it in the James 1:2-4 passage. Peter also says this in 1 Peter 1:6-7, "In this you *rejoice*, though now for a little while, if necessary, you have been grieved by various *trials*, so that the *tested* genuineness of your faith…may be found to result in praise and glory and honor at the revelation of Jesus Christ." This would be a good place to clarify what trials are and their purposes.

Trials Strengthen Your Faith

Think about lifting weights. When we lift weights, we challenge our muscles by putting them under stress. After a workout, our muscle fibers break down but are stimulated to build back stronger. This is a similar concept to stress roots and trees. Likewise, trials are challenging circumstances in life in which we exercise our faith in Jesus. Trials break us down to build us back up stronger. James says these trials come in various kinds (James 1:2). What are these various trials?

Sometimes, trials happen to us. Chronic pain, health struggles, car breaking down, stressful jobs, strained finances, rebellious children, and natural disasters. These are examples of things that happen to us that we have no control over. But God allows them so that we can exercise our faith and rely on Him. You can withstand current trials because of the trials you've endured in the past.

Also, trials come because of our faith. If you're a faithful follower of Jesus, suffering will follow you. Think about it like this: if you suffer for doing the right thing, you are doing something right. People will hate you, call you names, make fun of you, dissociate, and discriminate against you. Brothers and sisters around the world are even being disowned by their families and thrown in prisons, and their lives are threatened. No matter the severity, these trials are good because they strengthen our faith, and Jesus even said we should rejoice because our reward in heaven will be great (Matthew 5:11-12).

However, sometimes we suffer because of our sins. These are not trials from God but natural consequences of our actions. Like Proverbs 6:27 says, "Can a man carry fire next to his chest and his clothes not be burned?" God has given us boundaries in Scripture so that we wouldn't suffer unnecessarily from sin. But, sometimes, we choose to play with fire, and we get burned, and there's no joy in that. The Puritan John Trapp once said, "In our suffering for Christ, there is joy, not so when we suffer for our sins."[96] But, even God can take our mistakes and use them for our good.

Trials Test How Strong Your Faith Is

Think back to lifting weights. Lifting weights is an exercise that makes us stronger, but it also reveals how strong we are. In high school and college, we would try to find our "max." Can you imagine the testosterone? Besides trying to show off, finding your max is helpful. You're able to see and measure your progress over time. You cannot know you've grown unless you test it. Likewise, trials strengthen our faith, but they can also test how strong our faith is.

Another way of thinking about it is the tests we took in school. All of us would study the curriculum and be tested on what we knew. School tests prove what you know, but tests in life prove what you *believe*. As Peter says, trials test the genuineness of our faith (1 Peter 1:7). Suffering draws a line in the sand to see if we will draw closer to Jesus or walk away from Him. Suffering reveals who is truly a believer and who isn't.

But also, if we are believers, suffering tests our theology. Do you believe God is good? Do you believe Jesus loves you? Do you believe God uses suffering for your good? Do you believe God cares for you? Do you believe God is sovereign and in control? Do you believe He has your best interest in mind? Do you believe you can trust Him? Do you believe Jesus' way is better than your way? Do you believe Jesus is enough?

The way we respond to suffering will reveal the answers to these questions. When we suffer, do we turn to our idols to self-medicate and comfort us, or do we turn to Jesus? When we suffer, do we try to fix it on our own, or do we trust Jesus to fix it for us? Tests reveal how much we actually trust Him with our lives.

With that, God will also test our obedience. I think of Abraham and Isaac going up Mount Moriah. God didn't want Abraham to sacrifice Isaac, but God wanted to *test* Abraham's faith (Genesis 22:1). As the story goes, Abraham passed the test! But, sometimes, we don't pass the test like Abraham. Sometimes, the test shows us where our faith is still weak. I think of Peter when he denied Jesus three times. Jesus told Peter that a test was coming and that he would fail, and Peter did fail. After Peter denied Jesus, it broke Peter, and he was so ashamed. But, after the resurrection, Jesus didn't condemn Peter for denying Him but restored Peter and loved him. God uses tests to help us grow and learn. We will pass some and fail more, but Jesus is with us through all of it. Sometimes, we can get frustrated while in a trial or test and feel like God doesn't care or He's not present. We think, *God, where are you?* But remember, God is always with you, and teachers are always silent during a test.

But some trials feel like they are too heavy for us. Well, that's because they probably are. The saying, "God doesn't give you more than you can handle," is absolute baloney. If you have a coffee mug, T-shirt, or picture on your wall that says that, please burn it. That is simply a lie. The truth is God will repeatedly give you more than you can handle. He does that on purpose. Why? Consider what faith is. Trust, reliance, dependence. So, what is going to build trust, reliance, and dependence? Circumstances that push us to trust, rely, and depend on God. Paul learned that lesson in a painful way.

Trials are Perfect for Jesus' Power

One time, Paul had what he called "a thorn in his flesh," which he says was a messenger of Satan (2 Corinthians 12:7). No one knows what this thorn was, whether it was a physical ailment, injury, or demonic torment. Whatever it was, Paul didn't want it anymore and asked the Lord three times to remove it. Do you know what Jesus' answer was? He said no. What? Really, Jesus? But that wasn't just Jesus' answer. Jesus gave Paul a reason. Jesus said, "My grace is sufficient for you, for my power is made perfect in weakness" (2 Corinthians 12:9).

Paul didn't respond by being disappointed or upset with Jesus. Instead, he boasted in Jesus! He replied, "Therefore I will boast all the more gladly of my weaknesses, so that the power of Christ may rest upon me. For the sake of Christ, then, I am content with weaknesses, insults, hardships, persecutions, and calamities. For when I am weak, then I am strong" (2 Corinthians 12:9-10). Paul learned the secret that suffering produces strength because the strength comes from Jesus. As Paul famously said concerning his suffering, "I can do all things through him who strengthens me" (Philippians 4:13). That reality gave Paul joy.

How many times have we asked the Lord to remove suffering from our lives, and He hasn't done it the way we wanted or in a timely manner we would have liked? But, like Paul, Jesus' grace is sufficient, and His power is made perfect in *your* weakness. Suffering is an opportunity for Jesus' power to work through you supernaturally. God will put you through suffering to help you grow and learn to surrender to Jesus. As Corrie Ten Boom said, "You can never learn that Christ is all you need until Christ is all you have."[97] And His work doesn't stop here.

SUFFERING SHAPES OUR CHARACTER

Samantha and I have a friend named Adrian who loves to grow plants. Not only does she love to grow plants, but she even gives plants as gifts! On numerous occasions, she's given us plants for our house. But I'm embarrassed to say that Samantha and I are serial plant killers. I promise not on purpose. We just forget to water them for a couple of days—or sometimes weeks. Okay, we're bad plant parents.

Reflecting on John 15 and the vines and branches, Adrian had a unique perspective about the passage I would naturally overlook since I know nothing about plants. At the beginning of the passage, Jesus says in John 15:1-2 "I am the true vine, and my Father is the vinedresser. Every branch in me that does not bear fruit he takes away, and every branch that does bear fruit he *prunes*, that it may bear more fruit." She pointed out the work of the Father's pruning.

She said pruning is an essential part of keeping a plant healthy. When branches have dying parts, the plant will send all of its energy and nutrients to keep them alive. But doing so prevents the rest of the plant from growing. Instead of thriving, the plant is just surviving. Also, the dying parts are prone to develop diseases, which could eventually kill the whole plant. But if you prune the plant by cutting off the dead or dying parts, it allows the plant to disburse the nutrients and energy to the entire plant and helps it grow and produce even more fruit. There are even specific seasons to prune plants. For example, grape vines are typically pruned between February and March. After Adrian shared this, I understood more of what Jesus said about what the Father does for us.

The Father's Pruning

The Father oversees the vine and branches, Jesus and His church. People who aren't producing fruit are dead branches not connected to the vine. If they are not removed, they will prevent the church from growing and even make it sick. Judas was a dead branch. He spent three years with the true vine (Jesus) and living branches (the disciples), but he didn't love Jesus or others. He only loved himself. He didn't produce good fruit either. The fruit we saw was stealing and greed (John 12:6). So, the Father removed him, like a dead branch.

In the same way, the Father will remove dead branches from His church for its health. We all must consider whether we are a dead or living branch. Am I connected to the true vine by putting my faith in Jesus? Am I producing good fruit or bad fruit in my life? Plainly, don't be a Judas.

For the living branches producing good fruit, we may not be dead branches, but we still have dead parts that need to be removed. These are remnants of our old selves that we are trying to keep alive by giving energy to dead habits, mindsets, and behaviors. These things prevent us from thriving in our faith and producing more good fruit. So, the Father examines our lives and prunes the flaws hindering us from growing in our faith. When you are in a season of suffering, you're likely in a pruning season.

Sometimes, when we're in a suffering season, we feel like God is angry at us or that He's punishing us for something. But rest assured, God is not punishing you; He's likely pruning you. Punishment is focused on paying for past actions; pruning focuses on producing future fruit. When Jesus died on the cross, He took your punishment for you, and that punishment was final. When you are suffering, you never have to wonder if God is punishing you. His pruning is never out of anger or disgust; it's purely out of love for you.

But pruning is often painful. Pruning is not an act of behavior modification; rather, it's a heart transformation. He has to change the deepest parts of us, so God uses trials to perform heart surgery. He cuts off the dead parts in our hearts so that we can flourish in our new selves. This is what it may look like:

- If the Father wants you to grow in humility, He may prune the pride in your heart by allowing you to fail or experience the loss of a job, health, or relationship.
- If the Father wants you to grow in love, He may prune the detest in your heart by placing people around you who are hard to love.
- If the Father wants you to grow in patience, He may prune the impatience in your heart by surrounding you with difficult people or making you wait for something you want.

- If the Father wants you to grow in compassion, He may prune the self-centeredness in your heart by allowing others closest to you to suffer.
- If the Father wants you to grow in faith, He may prune the lack of faith in your heart by having you go through uncertain circumstances where you have to rely on Him.
- If the Father wants you to grow in forgiveness, He may prune the resentment in your heart by allowing you to be hurt by others.
- If the Father wants you to grow in generosity, He may prune the greed in your heart by losing money or resources that you stored up for yourself instead of giving to others.
- If the Father wants you to grow in integrity, He may prune the dishonesty in your heart by exposing your lies and what you've been hiding from others.
- If the Father wants you to grow in self-control, He may prune the self-indulgence in your heart by causing you to develop a health condition or encounter financial struggles.
- If the Father wants you to grow in gratitude, He may prune the entitlement in your heart by taking things away you care about the most so that you appreciate the blessings you do have.
- If the Father wants you to grow in peace, He may prune the worry in your heart by sending chaotic circumstances where you have to trust Him and not your own understanding.

Now, I'm not saying this is exactly what happens. God's reasons and ways are more complex than I can present. But it gives you an idea of how God prunes and what He's trying to achieve. His pruning is always purposeful. As Paul says, suffering produces endurance, and endurance produces *character* (Romans 5:4). Not that God wants us just to have good moral character; we want us to have *godly* character. The Father uses our circumstances and suffering to shape us into the characteristics of His Son. Other places in Scripture call this *refining*.

The Refining Fire

Refining is the process goldsmiths use to purify gold or silver. They put the metal in the fire, heat it until it is liquid, pull it out, and all the impurities rise to the top (called scum, draws). They scrape the impurities away, then they put the metal back in the furnace and repeat the process. The goldsmith knows the metal is pure once he can see the reflection of his face in the metal. Likewise, the Father will put us through fiery trials (1 Peter 1:6) to remove the impurities and imperfections in our hearts, and over time, we will reflect the image and character of His Son.

Just for a second, imagine what your life would look like if you were more humble, loving, gentle, kind, generous, peaceful, self-controlled, honest, forgiving, and compassionate. That sounds like you would be a whole lot more joyful because you would be a whole lot more like Jesus, and He's the most joyful being in heaven and earth! The reason many of us are not joyful in trials is because we are resistant to God's pruning. There are parts of our lives that we want to stay the same, or we don't like the way God is trying to change us. But when we submit to

God's pruning, we can consider it pure joy when we face trials because God is making us pure, like Jesus. We can have joy not only because we're becoming like Him but also because we have hope that we will spend eternity with Him.

SUFFERING ENDS WITH HOPE

A few years ago, Ellie and I were working on a puzzle together. She was having some trouble and was beginning to get frustrated. I noticed she was trying to put the puzzle together without looking at the picture on the box. I told her, "Honey, you have to look at the box to know where the pieces go." She replied, "I do it!" in her angry three-year-old voice. That was her way of saying, "Whatever, Dad, I'm going to do it my way!" Boy, I'm in trouble. Anyways, after a meltdown, Ellie finally let me help her. She finally looked at the picture on the box, and the pieces began to make sense to her. After she finished the puzzle, she was full of joy!

Similarly, we go through trials in life that just don't make sense. It's as if our trials are puzzle pieces, and we don't know what to do with them or how they fit into God's plan for our lives. *Why this way, God?* Your puzzle piece might be a hurt one. A grieving one. A doubtful one. A confused one. A strong one. Maybe even a joyful one. My encouragement to you is that there is hope for the piece you hold. You may only see the piece, but God sees the picture, and we can trust Him.

Joy and Sorrow

Peter says we shouldn't be surprised when trials come like something weird is happening to us (1 Peter 4:12). Why? Because we live in a broken world, with broken people and broken bodies. We should expect suffering to happen, especially as believers. But even though we shouldn't be surprised when trials happen, some trials do catch us by surprise. Trials are not on our calendars and are often tragic and traumatic. But, even in these times, God still has a purpose.

Now, even though we believe God is using our suffering for a purpose, it doesn't automatically remove the emotions we have about the situation. I think there is a misconception about joy in suffering that needs to be said. Having joy in suffering does not mean we don't have other emotions either. We are supposed to be sad and mourn when something tragic happens. It's okay to be angry and upset with God. We naturally are afraid or anxious when we are unsure about the future. Sometimes, other emotions are going to be stronger than our joy. For example, Samantha and I weren't jumping for joy in the ultrasound room the day we found out our baby passed away. Instead, we were devastated and struck with deep sadness. God doesn't want us to suppress or deny our emotions, but He wants us to feel them and deal with them with Him. Lamenting to God is a biblical practice we are warranted to do when we are hurting.

But just because we feel other emotions doesn't mean joy is absent. For believers, joy is supernatural when we abide in Jesus. It doesn't come from within ourselves; it comes from Him. That means we can be sorrowful and joyful simultaneously. That makes us different than any other people on the planet. That's what makes us people who are marked by joy.

For believers, mourning and joy are interwoven because they are both rooted in love. We cry tears of mourning because we won't see our loved one tomorrow, but we cry tears of joy *because we know* we'll see them again someday in heaven. Like what Paul said, "sorrowful, yet always *rejoicing*" (2 Corinthians 6:10). Why? Because we love and we have *hope*. Tim Keller once said, "The opposite of joy is not sorrow but *hopelessness*."[98] In other words, you won't have joy if you don't have hope. But, as long as we have hope, we will have joy. And for believers, there is always hope.

Paul says in Romans 5:4-5, "Character produces *hope*, and *hope* does not put us to shame." One of the classic verses used to give us hope is Romans 8:28, which says, "And we know that for those who love God all things work together for good, for those who are called according to his purpose." Although, when we are suffering, this verse is hard to believe, isn't it? Let's be honest: not "all things" feel like it's for our good. Being harassed, watching family members suffer and die of cancer, getting laid off at work, or hurricanes destroying your entire city and home are things that don't feel like they are for our good. And when things don't feel good, we start to question if God is good. We think, *God, why is this happening? God, what are you doing?* We feel this way because these things are painful, but also because these things were not a part of our plans.

When Life Wrecks Your Plans

When I think of this, I think of the story of Joseph in Genesis. Many things happened in his life that definitely were not in his 10-year plan. When he was 17, his brothers wanted to kill him but decided to sell him into slavery instead (that was so kind of them). He eventually finds himself in Egypt and is bought by

Potiphar, the officer of Pharaoh. While there, Potiphar's wife tried to seduce Joseph, but he ran away (way to go!). Out of frustration, Potiphar's wife falsely accused Joseph and charged him with rape. He was then thrown into Pharaoh's prison and was left and forgotten for many years. Notice Joseph suffered unjustly after obeying God and doing the right thing. That will happen, folks.

Many years passed, and a major turn of events happened. Pharaoh was having weird dreams. Word got to Pharaoh that Joseph, who was in prison, could interpret them. And he did! Because of Joseph's wisdom, Pharaoh appointed him second in command over all of Egypt. He was 17 when he was sold and 30 when he was appointed over Egypt. He spent all of his 20s in prison for something he did not do. That was definitely not a part of his plans. But all of this happened for a reason.

Shortly after being appointed, a huge famine took place in the land. Joseph's family was desperate and came to Egypt for help. When the brothers came to Joseph, they didn't recognize him, but he recognized them. After keeping his identity concealed and toying with them, Joseph eventually revealed himself, and the brothers thought they were dead meat. But Joseph's response to them was profound. He said to his brothers, "Do not fear, for am I in the place of God? As for you, you meant evil against me, but God meant it for *good*, to bring it about that many people should be kept alive, as they are today" (Genesis 50:19-20). Being sold into slavery, being wrongly accused of a crime he didn't commit, and being forgotten in prison for thirteen years was not a part of Joseph's plans, but it was a part of *God's plan*. All the bad things that happened to Joseph and the suffering he endured were intended for his future good and, ultimately, the good of other people. God does the same thing with us today.

God's Plan for Your Life

You've probably heard the saying, "Man plans, and God laughs." I know it's a tongue-in-cheek saying, but I don't think that's true. God doesn't take pleasure in watching us suffer. He also doesn't take pleasure in watching us get hurt when life doesn't go according to our plans. But, if we're honest, we hold our plans pretty tightly, don't we? We get upset when God doesn't fulfill daily, weekly, monthly, yearly, 5-year, 10-year, and 30-year plans. But God isn't obligated to make our plans happen. We're supposed to hold our plans loosely and submit to the plans He has for us. Proverbs 19:21 says, "Many are the plans in the mind of a man, but it is the purpose of the Lord that will stand." God knows the plans and purposes He has for our lives because He's written our stories. We're the ones finding out in real-time. Although some things happen that are not what we would have chosen, we can take comfort in knowing that they are for a purpose and for good.

We often say that God has a plan for your life. That is true. But actually, what is truer is that your life is a part of God's plan—His plan to redeem the world back to Himself. Before time began, God looked at all of history, and He chose you to be born in this time period, in your family, in this part of the world, to go to school where you go to school, to work at your job, and to have the friends you have. He also chose for you to endure the suffering you have endured, to make the mistakes that you have made, to trust in Jesus when you did, and eventually die when you will die and how you will die. God plans all of these things so that you will be conformed to the image of Christ and be used to bring others to Him.

When we get to the end of the Bible, the redemption story doesn't end. The plan and story continue. You are living in it right now! And when we see the big picture one day in glory, your life will be in God's storybook of the redemption of the world along with everyone before you and after you. God has a plan for your life, but your life is also a part of God's plan. All the work God is doing in you is for the work He is doing in the world. That's why we have hope. Even when it's hard, we have hope that God is using it and is with us through all of it.

God's Love in Our Suffering

Paul says we have hope because "God's love has been poured into our hearts through the Holy Spirit who has been given to us" (Romans 5:5). Suffering provides opportunities to experience God's love in a different way than you ever have before. You can only experience the love of the Healer when you're hurt, the love of the Provider when you are in need, the love of the Counselor when you're broken-hearted, the love of a Comforter until you're grieving, and the love of a Physician when you're sick. I can speak from my life experience that the closest I have ever been with God is in seasons of suffering. The Holy Spirit is in us to let us know it's going to be okay.

Then, in the same way we are loved and comforted by God, we are to do the same for others. 2 Corinthians 1:4-5 says God, "who comforts us in all our affliction, so that we may be able to comfort those who are in any affliction, with the comfort with which we ourselves are comforted by God. For as we share abundantly in Christ's sufferings, so through Christ we share abundantly in comfort too." Sometimes, part of God's plan is for us to go through suffering so that we can help others go through their suffering. For Samantha and me, several couples went through the same thing we did, and it helped us walk through our grief. They could empathize with us in ways no one else could because they experienced the pain themselves. Suffering connects us to others and eventually becomes a part of our story and ministry. Today, Samantha and I have helped other couples the same way others helped us and shared God's love and hope with them. The bottom line is that we are not meant to suffer alone. We need each other, and God designed us that way. It is our God-given purpose to love, comfort, and give people hope.

God also uses our suffering to advance the gospel. When apostles endured suffering, if it advanced the gospel in any way, they rejoiced in it! When Paul was imprisoned in Rome, he rejoiced because it advanced the gospel incredibly (Philippians 1:12). The whole imperial guard was getting saved because they were stuck with Paul every day, and all he would talk about was Jesus. Sometimes, the purpose of our suffering is so that someone else can come to know Jesus and the gospel. And we can rejoice in that just like the apostles did.

God's Glory at the End

The apostles also rejoiced because they knew the glory that was coming. Peter said, "But rejoice insofar as you share Christ's sufferings, that you may also rejoice and be glad when his glory is revealed" (1 Peter 4:13). No matter how our lives turn out, whether we heal or not, whether we have a lot or little, whether we live to a hundred or die young, no matter what, we *win*.

Paul says it this way: "We are more than conquerors through him who loved us" (Romans 8:37). "More than conquerors" is one Greek word, and it's a word that Paul made up to describe us. *Hypernikeo,* broken down, is *hyper,* which means "super" and *nikeo* which means "victor" or "conqueror." Nikeo is actually where the brand NIKE based its name. So, Paul says Christians are super-conquerors! You may ask, what's the difference between a regular conqueror and a super-conqueror? Regular conquerors rejoice when the battle is over. A super-conqueror rejoices in the midst of the battle because they know they are going to win. What will we defeat? *Death.*

We won't beat death because of anything we did, but only because Jesus beat it for us. And by placing our faith in Jesus, we have the assurance of our salvation. No matter how bad life gets here, you and I have a home in heaven waiting for us, and we will finally meet our Lord face-to-face. Through all our trials, once we realize that Jesus is our great treasure, our joy becomes unbreakable and eternal. He is who we cling to and long for. No matter how much we lose in life, we win in the end because of Jesus. One day, we'll be in paradise with Him where there is no more pain, no more tears, and no more heartache. Everything that we have lost will be restored and redeemed eternally. We will be rewarded for our suffering and service in the gospel. We will all be reunited with the ones we love, especially with our true love, Jesus. That's why all of us can be filled with an inexpressible glorious joy (1 Peter 1:8) because we belong to Jesus and will be with Him forever. This is why we can have joy in our suffering.

REFLECTION AND DISCUSSION QUESTIONS

1. In what ways do you try and build a "bubble" to avoid the possibility of suffering?
2. What's a time that you endured suffering that made your faith stronger?
3. Have you gone through pruning seasons before? How did you become more like Jesus as a result?
4. Has God used your suffering for good and His glory? How have you helped other people?
5. How do you respond when life doesn't go according to your plans? What can you do to adjust your mindset so that you are more open to God's plans?
6. How much does your eternal assurance affect your daily joy?

CHAPTER TEN

Joy is Contagious

What do you first think of when you hear the word *contagious*? I don't know about you, but the first thing I think of is a virus. Remember COVID? Of course, you do. It was awful! The whole world shut down for two years in a panic because public officials thought COVID-19 was going to be highly contagious and dangerous. In hindsight, COVID was pretty contagious. Just in the U.S. alone, one-third of the population contracted it.[99] Did you ever get it? I had it twice because I'm extra special. At least, that's what I tell myself. To this day, popcorn still doesn't taste right.

Now, I don't want to bum us out with bad memories, considering people passed away, businesses closed, students' education was ruined, and people went crazy. Never in my life did I think I would have to fight someone for toilet paper. What a time to be alive. Besides, viruses are not the only things that are contagious.

One of the most contagious things besides viruses is yawning. Yes, seriously. Anytime someone yawns by you, you'll likely yawn, too. Even the mention of yawning makes you want to yawn. As you read this, you've probably already yawned! And if you haven't yawned yet, come on, just give in. You know you want to. I feel like I just did a Jedi mind trick. Yawn, you will.

Also, laughing is contagious. Do you have a family member or friend whose laugh is infectious? As soon as they start laughing, you automatically laugh, too. You'll be sitting around the table laughing with friends and family, and no one can stop. Then you laugh so hard that it makes you cry or hurt your stomach. Honestly, laughing is a free and fun ab workout. Or it exposes your weak bladder. Hey, there's no shame here. I've been there.

Do you know what else is contagious? *Joy.*

Infectious Joy

When a person is marked by joy, people notice, and it's infectious. A joyful person is genuinely excited to see people and greet them with a big smile. Their words are always kind, encouraging, and life-giving. They are generous with their time and money and love to give gifts. They are enthusiastic about serving and invite others to join them. They aren't afraid to ask for help and enjoy the company when they have it. Everything they do is to please God, not to please people. They love Jesus and love others with their whole heart. They are a great friend, and you can always count on them. To put it into one word, joyful people *shine.*

Jesus once said in John 8:12, "I am the light of the world. Whoever follows me will not walk in darkness but will have the light of life." This statement is part of the seven "I Am" statements Jesus made about Himself uniquely in John's Gospel. What's especially unique about this particular I Am statement is that it's the only one where Jesus calls us the same thing. In Matthew 5:14-16, Jesus says, "*You* are the light of the world. A city set on a hill cannot be hidden. Nor do people light a lamp and put it under a basket, but on a stand, and it gives light to all in the house. In the same way, let your light *shine* before others so that they may see your good works and give glory to your Father who is in heaven." Jesus tells us to shine.

A person marked by joy isn't influenced by their environment; rather, they influence it. Just like darkness can't overcome light, light always dispels darkness. Their joy radiates through the room, and people are drawn to them. People are warmed by their love. Their joy gives other people joy.

So why does Jesus call us to shine? He says, "so that they may see your good works and give glory to your Father who is in heaven" (Matthew 5:16). Our purpose in shining is so that other people can see and know God. Doing good works with joy is evangelistic.

When I think of the radiance of joy, I think of the connection joy has with other words such as grace, gifts, and thanksgiving. In Greek, each of these words shares the same root, *char*. Take a look:

>*char*isma- Gifts
>*char*is- Grace
>eu*char*isteo- Thanksgiving
>*char*a- Joy

If you think about it, their connection makes sense. Together, they create a gospel chain reaction as we engage with God and His goodness. God is so generous to us. Everything that we have is a *gift* from Him. But the greatest gift God gives us is his *grace*, which is His unmerited favor. He always gives us what we do not deserve, most notably our salvation. We aren't saved by our own efforts, good works, or church attendance, but we are saved by grace through faith in Jesus (Ephesians 2:8). That's the greatest gift in the world! That's why our response to that amazing grace is *thanksgiving*. We are thankful to the Father for all the blessings in our lives, but especially thankful for sending Jesus to save us. We are thankful to Jesus for dying for our sins in our place and offering us eternal life. And because we receive and live in God's grace and have thankful hearts, we have *joy*. When we rejoice in the gospel, we shine bright.

But the gospel isn't something we're to just enjoy for ourselves. We are called to share the gospel with others. We do that by engaging people the way God engaged us. We are to shine just like He shines. We must be generous to others just like God is generous to us. We must give people grace as God has given us grace. We must be incredibly thankful to others like we are thankful to God. We must be joyful like God is joyful, and we want others to know Him.

This was true for the apostles and the early believers. They were full of joy because of the gospel. They were free from a Law they couldn't keep and free from the sin they were enslaved to. But ultimately, they rejoiced because they finally could have a relationship with the living God through Jesus. Because of that, they devoted their lives to Jesus, the church, and the gospel message. They wanted others to know Him so they could be saved and have joy as well.

Many people rejoiced in receiving Christ throughout the apostle's ministry, but others rejected Christ and were angry. That's going to happen because people love darkness more than light (John 3:19). But even when the gospel cost the apostles and other believers their relationships and businesses and caused them to experience discrimination and persecution, they still rejoiced! Why? Because no hardship could take Jesus away from them. Nothing could put out the fire of their joy in the gospel; it only fueled it. And as they shared the gospel with joy, it spread like wildfire. Joy is supernaturally contagious because the gospel is supernaturally contagious.

When you have joy, you have what other people want. It's like when you have a new gadget or product, someone will say, "Hey, where did you get that?" 95% of the time, it's Amazon. But you can't buy joy on Amazon. So, when you abide in Jesus and joy marks your life, people will notice and wonder, "Why do you have so much joy?" And given the opportunity, we won't tell them where to get joy or how to have joy. Instead, we will tell them who gives us joy. Joy is not just infectious; it's an invitation. Let me introduce you to the one who gives me joy. His name is Jesus.

Likewise, if we are professing Christians and are not joyful, unbelievers are not going to be interested in the gospel because we are no different than anyone else. Being a miserable Christian is a terrible witness. That's why we need to be deeply connected to Jesus and others so joy can supernaturally flow through us. That will get people's attention and make them curious. As A.W. Tozer once said, "The Christian owes it to the world to be supernaturally joyful."[100]

So, if the gospel itself gives us joy and sharing the gospel gives us joy, how well are we doing? Are we as devoted to the gospel as the first-century Christians? Are we motivated to share the gospel, even if it costs us? Overall, studies show that the American church is not doing well.

The Church and Evangelism

In 2022, Lifeway Research conducted a study on evangelism sampling self-identified Christians. The study revealed that in a six-month period, 46% reported sharing a Bible verse or their story with an unbeliever, 43% invited an unbelieving friend or family member to a church service, and 38% discussed how to become a Christian with an unbeliever.[101] Those findings were confirmed in another study sampling 2000 American unbelievers. The study showed two-thirds have multiple Christian friends (Avg. 3-4). Of that group, a discouraging 70% have never heard the gospel from any of their Christian friends.[102] Let that sink in for a second. The majority of Christians are not sharing the gospel with their unbelieving friends. If that wasn't discouraging enough, another study showed that two-thirds of Americans expressed they are "open or very open" to discussing the Christian faith with a friend.[103] In other words, people are open to a gospel conversation, but most Christians aren't starting the conversation.

Can this be true? Well, do a self-evaluation using the same criteria. In the last six months, have you shared your story or a Bible verse with an unbeliever? Have you invited an unbeliever to church? Have you shared the gospel with an unbeliever and how to be saved?

Jesus said in Matthew 28:19-20, "Go therefore and make disciples of all nations, baptizing them in the name of the Father and of the Son and of the Holy Spirit, teaching them to observe all that I have commanded you. And behold, I am with you always, to the end of the age." This is the great commission, and it should be the mission of every believer and church. The great commission is not a great suggestion; it's a command. If we are not actively making disciples personally or as a local church, then we are being disobedient to our Lord. And Jesus told us we will be held accountable to His command. In Matthew 25, with the parable of the talents, every believer will give an account for their service in the gospel. When we stand before Jesus, believers will either be rewarded and full of rejoicing, or they will be rebuked and full of regret. We must take this command seriously because Jesus takes this seriously.

Our lack of evangelism also reveals another reason why many of us lack joy. We're neglecting a fundamental and foundational part of what it means to be a follower of Jesus. As a pastor, people who meet with me often say, "I feel stagnant in my faith" or "I just don't feel close to God." Naturally, I would ask them about their Bible reading habits and what their prayer life is like. Those things are important, but I also think we need to ask about their evangelism and service. What are you doing to serve the Lord daily? Who are you actively pursuing the gospel with? Who are you discipling? Let me be clear: sharing the gospel and discipling others is as foundational as reading your Bible and praying. If you aren't evangelizing and discipling others, you will lack joy because you're not abiding in Jesus.

But here's the good news: you can change that today! An encouraging detail from the studies shows that unbelievers are open to gospel conversations. As Jesus said, the harvest is plentiful, but the workers are few (Matthew 9:34). Now I recognize it's easier said than done. Many of us are afraid to share the gospel with others. We're afraid of saying something wrong or not knowing how they will respond. Some of us may feel inadequate or ill-equipped to share the gospel. You may be unsure how to engage in a gospel conversation. Believe me, I understand. I've been there. So, with this fear and uncertainty in mind, I want to look at an example in Scripture that will help us take steps to grow in our evangelism and unlock a joy that may be lacking. We're going to look at a guy named Philip.

Philip the Evangelist

In the New Testament, two notable men were named Philip. There was Philip the Apostle and Philip the Evangelist. Sometimes, people mistakenly think these Philips are the same person, but they are different individuals. For this chapter, we will look at Philip the Evangelist.

Philip is first introduced as one of the seven deacons appointed by the apostles in Acts 6:5. He was chosen because he loved Jesus and the church and had a heart to serve. What I love about Philip is that he was just a normal person like you and me. He was a faithful servant, taking care of others in need. However, Philip also had a burning passion for evangelizing, which is why he is known as Philip the Evangelist. He got his nickname because of what he did in Acts 8, where we will focus our attention. We can learn a lot about evangelism from Philip.

From the beginning, we see in Philip's ministry that wherever he went to preach the gospel, the people were filled with *joy*. When the church began to be persecuted in Jerusalem, many believers scattered. When that happened, Philip went to Samaria, just north of Judea. Samaria was often a place Jews avoided because of prejudice and racism. During that time, Jews and Samaritans hated each other. But despite the tension, Philip went to Samaria and preached the gospel, performed miracles, and healed many people. When Philip left, "there was much *joy* in that city" (Acts 8:8).

Later in the chapter, God has a different mission for Philip. Instead of pursuing people with the gospel, God wanted him to pursue a person. From this interaction, we can learn a lot about how we can engage in personal evangelism. Whether it's a family member, good friend, neighbor, or stranger, we can apply the principles we see in Philip.

In Acts 8:26-27, it says, "Now an angel of the Lord said to Philip, 'Rise and go toward the south to the road that goes down from Jerusalem to Gaza.' This is a desert place. And he rose and went." We see that God sends Philip to a place called Gaza, which is described as a desert. Gaza was not pleasant, but ironically, it was close to the beach. Thanks a lot, God! Why couldn't you send me to the beach instead of the desert?

Luke adds this detail about Gaza for a reason. Sometimes, God sends us to unpleasant places, situations, or jobs or to engage with unpleasant people. But maybe what God is having you do is not about you but about accomplishing His mission *through* you. Candidly, too often, we think the world revolves around us. But we are a part of something greater than ourselves, advancing the gospel and building the kingdom of God. Philip understood this, and that's why he got up and went. Philip showed the first principle in personal evangelism, to be obedient.

1. Be Obedient

Philip did not hesitate when the angel said *go*. He arose and went. Notice the message from the Lord didn't have any other details besides telling Philip, "Go to Gaza." That's because often God doesn't give us the whole plan; rather, He gives us a task. As we go through our day, the Holy Spirit will give us a thought that sounds like this: Go talk to that person. Go buy that coworker lunch. Go help your neighbor with the yard. Go pay for that person's coffee. Go encourage that grocery store employee. The Holy Spirit still says go today because He is still at work and wants to use you! But our problem is that we say *no* when He says go.

There are several reasons why we say no. At the moment, we'll think, "That's going to be awkward," or "I don't have time for that right now," or "What if I offend them?" or "I don't know what to say," or "I'm not gifted in sharing the gospel." So, what do we do? We avoid, walk away, look down, or pull out our phones. When we say no, we are full of escape plans and excuses. When we do that, we rob ourselves of being used by God, which is robbing ourselves of joy and the potential of giving someone else joy, too.

So what if we turned our no into a *yes*? Anytime the Spirit says go, it's never insignificant. Ephesians 2:10 says, "For we are his workmanship, created in Christ Jesus for good works, which God prepared beforehand, that we should walk in them." When the Spirit says go, He's set something up supernatural for you to do.

Paul gives us a picture of what this looks like as we work with God in evangelism and discipleship. Paul said to the Corinthian church, "I planted, Apollos watered, but God gave the growth," and later, "He who plants and he who waters are one, and each will receive his wages according to his labor. For we are God's fellow workers" (1 Corinthians 3:6, 8-9). Paul explains that evangelism and discipleship are like spiritual farming. Paul was the missionary who sowed the seeds of the gospel and planted the church in Corinth. Apollos was the pastor of the church after Paul left and was responsible for watering and nurturing the seeds that were planted. And no matter their efforts, the growth belonged to God. This picture Paul painted is still true today.

As followers of Jesus, we are fellow workers with God. Our role is to plant and water seeds of the gospel as the Spirit leads us. We don't have to worry about the outcome because that belongs to God. He's in charge of the growth. With that in mind, there may be people in our lives that we're close to who aren't following Jesus or who haven't grown in their faith the way we'd liked. That can be discouraging. You've tried sharing the gospel repeatedly but don't see the needle moving. But remember, God is in charge of their growth, not you. Your role is to faithfully sow and water seeds of the gospel with your actions, words, and prayers.

So every day, when the Spirit says go, He's calling you to sow and water seeds of the gospel. You may sow a seed in someone for the first time, or you may water a seed someone else planted days, months, or years ago. Or a seed you've sowed in someone is being watered by others. The point is that evangelism is a team effort. God is the one supernaturally orchestrating everything; we all have to play our part.

Anytime you name-drop Jesus, do an act of kindness, or give an encouraging word, you're getting that person one step closer to Jesus. That is never insignificant. The task may seem small or even scary to you, but in the end, it may be life-changing for someone. You may get to heaven someday and meet someone you said, "Jesus loves you," after you have helped them. They may have been wrestling with Jesus' existence and asked for a sign, and you were the sign! That's how God works. So we should go throughout the day eager and joyful to sow and water seeds of the gospel as the Spirit leads us. When God says go, don't say no; say yes.

When Philip said yes to God, he discovered why God sent him to Gaza. Acts 8:27-28 says, "And there was an Ethiopian, a eunuch, a court official of Candace, queen of the Ethiopians, who was in charge of all her treasure. He had come to Jerusalem to worship and was returning, seated in his chariot, and he was reading the prophet Isaiah." In the distance, Philip saw this man, but he wasn't just any ordinary man. He was an Ethiopian eunuch. Now, during that time, Ethiopia was considered the ends of the earth. A round trip from Ethiopia to Jerusalem would take a hundred days. Can you imagine? I hear my five-year-old saying, "Are we there yet?" Nope, forty days still to go.

But this man wasn't just Ethiopian. He was also a eunuch. Likely, his lack of body hair and small stature would have signified to Philip that he was a eunuch, which again would have been unusual. Then, to cap off the uniqueness of this man, this Ethiopian eunuch was a high-ranking government official, the treasurer for the Queen of Ethiopia. In other words, this man was rich, powerful, and had status. He rode in a chariot, equivalent to riding in a limo today. He traveled in luxury, which may have made the long journey a little bit more tolerable.

So why was this rich foreign government official in Gaza, of all places? Shouldn't he be at the beach on vacation? No. He was just in Jerusalem to worship. What's interesting is that he wasn't Jewish; he was a Gentile. In those days, this man would be described as a "Gentile God-fearer." In other words, he was someone searching to know and worship the God of Jews. Which, if you think about it, would also be unusual. How did he know about the God of the Jews? He's from Ethiopia, where the people were pagan. This means that someone was faithful enough to sow a seed in this man at some point in his life. And now he was searching for answers about God.

Unfortunately for the eunuch, he would have gone to the temple in Jerusalem and been rejected. Gentiles weren't allowed to worship in the temple, especially no eunuchs. How heartbreaking that must have been. He traveled so far to be turned away. Likely disheartened, he left Jerusalem, and now he is in the desert, reading a Bible that he bought, still searching for God. Then, Philip shows up.

Acts 8:29-30 says, "And the Spirit said to Philip, 'Go over and join this chariot.' So Philip ran to him, heard him reading Isaiah the prophet, and asked, 'Do you understand what you are reading?' And he said, 'How can I unless someone guides me?' And he invited Philip to come up and sit with him." Notice that the Spirit gave Philip another go! When you're faithful with one task, God will give you another one. For Philip, he was so quick to go that he ran! When he got to the chariot, his ears perked up, and he heard the eunuch reading Scripture. Then Philip engages the eunuch with a question, which is the next key principle for us.

2. Ask Questions

The best way to approach someone who has questions about life is to ask questions. Jesus was the king of this. To be exact, in the Gospels, Jesus asked 307 questions and was asked 183 questions but only answered 8. When Jesus was asked a question, he would often turn it around and ask the person a question. As Martin B. Copenhaver says, "It seems clear that Jesus prefers to be the one asking the questions. Jesus is more than forty times more likely to ask a question than to answer one directly."[104] Now, Jesus' question asking may have frustrated people, especially disciples. But He wasn't trying to be elusive; He was being strategic.

Jesus modeled for us that we shouldn't lecture people. Instead, ask questions that lead people to the answers they are looking for. Self-realization is far greater than lecture, and asking questions facilitates that experience. Also, while asking questions, you get to know the person. You learn what matters most to them and understand what they think and believe and why they've come to their conclusions.

Philip asked the eunuch if he understood what he was reading (Acts 8:30). Philip asked that question because he wanted to know where the eunuch was spiritually. Likewise, we should also ask others spiritual questions because those questions matter most. Asking spiritual questions reveals if the person knows Jesus and is following Him. And if they aren't, asking questions will help you know why. Spiritual questions also reveal where they are hurting and what needs they may have, which can guide you to help meet their physical, emotional, and spiritual needs.

Spiritual conversations are not typically served on a silver platter like Philip and the eunuch. Sometimes, you have to start with common ground questions that move to personal questions that lead to spiritual questions. Here are some examples:

Common Ground Questions: Hey, that's a cool shirt; where'd you get that? Do you like sports? How long have you lived in the area? Do you read books? Any good recommendations? Do you listen to any podcasts? Are you watching any shows right now?

Personal Questions: How's the family? Where'd you grow up? What's your story? What's been your greatest *joy* in life? What's been your biggest struggle in life? Who's been the most influential person in your life? What are your goals?

Spiritual Questions: Do you go to church anywhere? Do you believe in God? What do you think your purpose is? What do you think about Jesus? How confident are you that you would go to heaven? If God asked you why He should let you in heaven, what would you say?

As we have conversations with people, we must intentionally move the conversation to spiritual instead of staying in the common ground or personal. For example, guys love to talk about sports, and that's perfectly fine. However, we tend to stay in our comfort zone and only talk about sports. Don't do that. In the end, sports are meaningless. Believe me, I'm a big sports fan and an ex-collegiate athlete. But the truth is talking about sports won't change eternity, but talking about the Savior will.

It's also imperative that while you're asking good questions, you are also a great listener. Because before your friends, family, coworkers, or strangers will listen to you, they want to see if you care enough to really listen to them. You have to earn the right to be heard. And when you ask good questions and listen well, you open the door for them to ask *you* questions. That's what the eunuch did. After Philip asked him if he understood what he was reading, the eunuch asked, *"How can I unless someone guides me"* (Acts 8:31)? The eunuch then invited Philip into his chariot, and they started to read the passage together.

Here's an important note to make. When people ask you questions, there will be times you won't know the answer. It's totally okay to say, "I don't know." But, commit to sit on the chariot with them and find the answer together. Don't run away when people ask you hard questions. Lean in and help them wrestle with God. Research and reach out to trusted believers for wisdom and insight. This will help sharpen you and build your faith as well.

When Philip and the eunuch were sitting on the chariot, the Scripture the eunuch was reading was a passage out of Isaiah 53:7-8. That specific passage was a prophecy about the Messiah who would be murdered unjustly. The Messiah wouldn't defend himself and was willing to die for others. After reading that, the eunuch was distraught. The eunuch asked Philip, "Who is this?" Ah, more questions! So, Philip goes on to answer the eunuch's question. Acts 8:35 says, "Then Philip opened his mouth, and beginning with this Scripture, he told him the good news about Jesus." Ready for this? Good questions lead to *good news*! The third key principle to personal evangelism is to share Jesus.

3. Share Jesus

Notice that it says Philip opened his mouth (Acts 8:35), which is important. This may be the most significant detail of this whole story. Because here's the thing: this is where we fumble the ball on the 1-yard line. We struggle to open our mouths and tell people about Jesus.

You may have heard the saying, "Share the gospel at all times and use words when necessary." I understand what it's saying. Your life should represent the gospel, and that will speak for itself. There is some truth to that. However, I think many of us use this mentality as an excuse not to open our mouths. I'd argue that opening your mouth and telling people about Jesus is *always necessary*.

A verse we love is Romans 10:13, which says, "For everyone who calls on the name of the Lord will be saved." But we forget the verse that comes right after in Romans 10:14, "How then will they call on him in whom they have not believed? And how are they to believe in him of whom they have never heard? And how are they to hear without someone preaching?" In other words, how can people believe in Jesus and call on His name *if no one tells them*? We have to open our mouths.

Philip opened his mouth, and *"beginning with the Scriptures he told him the good news about Jesus"* (Acts 8:35). It just so happened that this passage from Isaiah 53 was a vivid description of Jesus' crucifixion prophesied 700 years before. The events Philip and the eunuch were reading about had just happened, and Philip likely witnessed all of it. But what seemed like bad news in Isaiah was actually good news. Philip shared with the eunuch that the death of Jesus was actually a *sacrifice*. What seemed like a defeat was actually a victory. Jesus took the death penalty for all people's sins, including the eunuch's. Now, Jesus offers forgiveness of sins and eternal life. And Philip used the Scripture and his testimony to share this good news.

I notice today that believers feel ill-equipped to share the gospel with others. But I want you to know you are equipped with the very same things Philip was that day with the eunuch. You have the Holy Spirit, the Scriptures, and your personal testimony. You can share key passages that outline the gospel, such as John 3:16, Romans 6:23, and Ephesians 2:8-9. Another classic and helpful gospel presentation is the Roman Road which is:

- Romans 3:23: "For all have sinned and fall short of the glory of God."
- Romans 6:23: "For the wages of sin is death, but the free gift of God is eternal life in Christ Jesus our Lord.
- Romans 10:9: "If you confess with your mouth that Jesus is Lord and believe in your heart that God raised him from the dead, you will be saved."

I encourage you to have these verses memorized or on your phone ready to go. Or, in addition to any of these verses, share verses that have deeply impacted your life. Even before writing this book, John 15:5 has been a life verse, and I share it with people often. It's important that when you are sharing Scripture, don't just start preaching at people. Present it as another question. Say, "Can I share with you some verses that have been meaningful to my life?" That allows them to give permission, and that helps them not feel pressured. Then, if they haven't already asked you,

you can say, "Can I share with you my story?" which leads to your personal testimony.

In the court of law, when you're a witness, your testimony is simply telling the truth about what you have seen and heard. As witnesses of Jesus, all we are called to do is tell people the truth about what Jesus has done in our lives. It's important not to ramble on for an hour about your story. Here are some helpful questions to help you structure your testimony.

1. Who were you before knowing Jesus?
2. How did you come to know Jesus?
3. How is your life different now that you are following Jesus?

It's good practice to keep your story to about two minutes. Just like a mock trial, practice telling it in a mirror or with friends or family. When you tell your story, it's important to talk about your struggles with sin; just don't glorify the sin. Telling people about how bad you were is dishonoring. I've seen that too often and it's cringy. But be honest about your struggles. Remember, people connect with our weaknesses. People can relate to struggle and heartache. So be real with them. People are attracted to authenticity. Most importantly, they'll be attracted to Jesus, who changed your life, because they'll want that too.

Depending on the relationship and the situation will determine how much time you have. If the person is a family member, friend, or coworker, you will have many times to sow and water gospel seeds, Lord willing. This type of evangelism is like a marathon. They will take time, and you'll have many opportunities to be obedient, ask questions, and share Jesus.

However, it's important to seize every opportunity. Build trust and earn the right to be heard by loving them well. And don't forget to open your mouth and talk about Jesus any chance you get. Also, just like a marathon, don't give up. Sow and water, the growth belongs to God.

There will be other times when the Spirit will lead you to engage with a stranger. This type of evangelism is not a marathon but a sprint. You have a very short time with them, so you must make the time you do have count. But no matter how the Spirit leads you, open your mouth and share Jesus. Even if you don't have time to ask questions and share your testimony, just drop Jesus' name. Whether it's after you help someone or when someone helps you, say something like "Jesus loves you," or "Jesus wanted me to do this for you," or "Jesus sees you and cares for you." Say His name. When you do, you're sowing and watering.

Also, ask if you can pray for people. Next time you visit a restaurant, ask if you can pray for your waiter or waitress. Or the next time you have a plumber, mechanic, pest control, or lawn care at your house, ask if you can pray for them. Then, pray for them on the spot. Seriously! They may say no, but you'll be surprised how many will say yes. Make that a habit in your life and see what God does with it.

Give Jesus glory and say His name no matter the situation or relationship! Otherwise, if we do something nice and don't say His name, we're no different than an atheist who does something nice. We'll also be tempted to steal the glory that belongs to Jesus. Don't be shy or ashamed; open your mouth and say His name!

So, how did the eunuch respond to the gospel? Acts 8:37-39 says, "And as they were going along the road they came to some water, and the eunuch said, 'See, here is water! What prevents me from being baptized?' And he commanded the chariot to stop, and they both went down into the water, Philip and the eunuch, and he baptized him. And when they came up out of the water, the Spirit of the Lord carried Philip away, and the eunuch saw him no more, and went on his way *rejoicing*."

The eunuch surrendered his life to Christ and received salvation. How awesome is that? As Philip and eunuch were riding along, they saw some water. Remember, this was a desert. There was no water around. But the Lord provided, and the eunuch eagerly wanted to get baptized. So they got out of the chariot, and Philip baptized him. Then it says the Lord took Philip onto his next mission, and the eunuch went back on his journey home *rejoicing*. Why was he rejoicing? Because he found what he was looking for. He found Jesus.

For the eunuch, he was in the royal court in the Ethiopian kingdom. In Jesus' kingdom, he was now in the royal family. Eternity changed for the eunuch, and he went home full of joy. There are so many people around us who are like the eunuch. They are searching for meaning, purpose, and joy. They may not know it, but what they are truly searching for is Jesus. We have the opportunity to invite them to know Him. And there is something extra special and joyful when you ask a person if they want to put their faith in Jesus, and their answer is *yes*.

Sometimes, God gives us the honor to reap the harvest of leading someone to Christ. A lot of times, we were reaping a seed we didn't sow. There may have been much sowing and watering before us, but we get to finish the mission. Likewise, others will reap seeds that we have sown, and that is awesome, too. Personally, the Lord has used me to sow, water, and reap, and I can say there is nothing more joyful than leading a brother or sister to Christ. Salvation is a joyful experience for the person leading and the person receiving, and all of heaven rejoices, too. As the missionary Lottie Moon once said, "Surely there can be no greater joy than that of saving souls."[105] With that being said, be obedient, ask questions, and share Jesus. Watch your joy become full.

CONCLUSION

In his book *Evangelism Is*, David Early wrote, "True joy does not reach its climax in private communion with God. Rather, it reaches its fullest extent only when it is compounded by the joy of seeing others share in it with us."[106] I'm so thankful you chose to join me on this joy journey. I pray this book has helped you be marked by joy, just like the first disciples. Now shine bright like Jesus and tell everyone around you how they can have joy, too.

REFLECTION AND DISCUSSION QUESTIONS

1. What about the gospel gives you joy? Does this realization give you daily joy?
2. When was the last time you led a person to Christ? What was that experience like?
3. Why do you think the American church is lacking in evangelism today?

4. What's your typical reasoning to say no when the Spirit say go? How can you turn your no into a yes?
5. How can you intentionally share Jesus everyday with people around you?
6. Who can you pray for that they would receive Christ?

Endnotes

1. Karen H. Jobes, *1 Peter*. Edited by Robert W. Yarbrough and Joshua Jipp, (Grand Rapids: Baker Publishing Group, 2022), 94-99.
2. Gallup. "Gallup 2023 Global Emotions Report." *Gallup*. https://www.gallup.com/analytics/507719/gallup%202023%20global%20emotions%20report.aspx
3. Oracle. "Global Report: 45% of People Have Not Felt True Happiness for More Than Two Years." *Oracle*. https://www.oracle.com/news/announcement/oracle-cx-happiness-research-study-2022-06-15/
4. CDC. "Anxiety and Depression: Household Pulse Survey." *CDC*. https://www.cdc.gov/nchs/covid19/pulse/mental-health.htm
5. National Center for Drug Abuse Statistics. "Drug Abuse Statistics." *National Center for Drug Abuse Statistics*. https://drugabusestatistics.org/
6. Centers for Disease Control and Prevention. "Suicide Data and Statistics." *Centers for Disease Control and Prevention*. https://www.cdc.gov/suicide/suicide-data-statistics.html

7. Wyatt, Tim. "91% of Christians say mental illness is stigmatized in the Church. But the solution may be simpler than you think." *Premiere Christianity*. April 22, 2022. https://www.premierchristianity.com/news-analysis/91-of-christians-say-mental-illness-is-stigmatised-in-the-church-but-the-solution-may-be-simpler-than-you-think/12924.article
8. John Mark Comer, *Ruthless Elimination of Hurry* (Colorado Springs: Water Brook, 2019), 24.
9. Yale Center for Faith and Culture at Yale Divinity School. "Theology of Joy and Good Living." *Yale Center for Faith and Culture at Yale Divinity School.* https://faith.yale.edu/legacy-projects/theology-of-joy
10. Piper, John. "The Fruit of Hope: Joy." *Desiring God.* https://www.desiringgod.org/messages/the-fruit-of-hope-joy
11. Warren, Kay. "Choose Joy Quotes." *Goodreads.* https://www.goodreads.com/work/quotes/24527409-choose-joy-because-happiness-isn-t-enough
12. John Mark Comer, *The Ruthless Elimination of Hurry*, 24.
13. Alcorn, Randy. "Is There a Difference Between Happiness and Joy?" *EPM.* https://www.epm.org/resources/2015/Nov/11/difference-happiness-joy/
14. Stephen D. Renn, *Expository Dictionary of Bible Words: Word Studies for Key English Bible Words Based on the Hebrew and Greek Texts*, (Peabody, Massachusetts: Hendrickson Publishers, 2005), 538-541.
15. Stephen D. Renn, *Expository Dictionary of Bible Words*, 541-542.
16. Ibid.

17. Tony Reinke, *12 Ways Your Phone is Changing You* (Wheaton: Crossway, 2017), 59.
18. Stephen D. Renn, *Expository Dictionary of Bible Words*, 498.
19. Joni Eareckson Tada, *Heaven: Your Real Home* (Grand Rapids: Zondervan, 1995), 39.
20. Piper, John. "The Fruit of Hope: Joy." *Desiring God.* https://www.desiringgod.org/messages/the-fruit-of-hope-joy
21. Pixar. "Inside Out." *Pixar.* https://www.pixar.com/feature-films/inside-out
22. Scarlet, Dr. Janina. "Inside Out: Emotional Truth by Way of Pixar," *Psychology Today.* June 24, 2015, https://www.psychologytoday.com/us/blog/beyond-heroes-and-villains/201506/inside-out-emotional-truths-way-pixar
23. Taylor, Jill Bolte. "Paul Ekman" *Time Magazine.* April 30, 2009. https://content.time.com/time/specials/packages/article/0,28804,1894410_1893209_1893475,00.html
24. Paul Ekman. "About Paul Ekman." *Paul Ekman.* https://www.paulekman.com/about/paul-ekman/
25. Paul Ekman. "Atlas of Emotions." *Paul Ekman.* https://www.paulekman.com/projects/atlas-of-emotions/
26. Johnson, Matthew Kuan. "Joy: a review of the literature and suggestions for future direction." *The Journal of Positive Psychology,* 2019. https://www.tandfonline.com/doi/full/10.1080/17439760.2019.1685581
27. B.L. Fredrickson, "What good are positive emotions?" *Review of General Psychology,* 2, 309.
28. Watkins, Philip. "Joy and Wellbeing." *George Mason University.* https://wellbeing.gmu.edu/joy-and-well-being/

29. National Library of Medicine. "The Genetic Links to Anxiety and Depression (GLAD) Study." *National Library of Medicine*. https://www.ncbi.nlm.nih.gov/pmc/articles/PMC6891252/
30. Philip C. Watkins, "Appraising joy" *The Journal of Positive Psychology*, 2019, 4.
31. Philip C. Watkins, "Appraising joy," 1.
32. Yale Center for Faith and Culture, "Theology of Joy: Robert Emmons with Matt Croasmun" YouTube, 05:30, September 25, 2014, https://www.youtube.com/watch?v=CxDOVQKKp5c&list=PLO-6cjKGDlet70bQZVjSyl5dsRWfCCSAn&index=7
33. Philip C. Watkins, "Appraising joy," 3.
34. Randy Alcorn, *Happiness*, (Carol Stream: Tyndale House, 2015), 39.
35. Ibid. 39.
36. D.L. Moody, *Heaven*, (Chicago: Moody Press, 1995), 47.
37. AW Tozer, *Who Put Jesus on the Cross?* (Camp Hill: WingSpread, 2009), e-book.
38. Randy Alcorn, *Happiness*, 39.
39. Fredrickson, Barbara. "The Role of Positive Emotions in Positive Psychology," https://www.ncbi.nlm.nih.gov/pmc/articles/PMC3122271/
40. IE University. "Cultivating Joy to Improve Well Being." *IE University*. https://www.ie.edu/insights/articles/cultivate-joy-to-improve-well-being/
41. U.S. Dept. of Health and Human Services. "The Epidemic of Loneliness and Isolation." *U.S. Dept. of Health and Human Services*. https://www.hhs.gov/sites/default/files/surgeon-general-social-connection-advisory.pdf

42. National Geographic, "King Tut's Treasures: Hidden Secrets Rediscovered," YouTube video, 04:10, November 26, 2023, https://youtu.be/VANTQdAm5eA?si=Z38QErcF9GOJ0L2g
43. Marrianne Meye Thompson. "Reflections on Joy in the Bible," Yale Center for Faith and Culture, Joy and Human Flourishing, September 2012.
44. Renn, *Expository Dictionary of Bible Words*, 538.
45. Piper, John. "The Fruit of Hope: Joy," https://www.desiringgod.org/messages/the-fruit-of-hope-joy
46. Alcorn, Randy. "Is Joy Unemotional, and Is It More Spiritual Than Happiness?" https://www.epm.org/resources/2016/Jul/20/joy-unemotional-happiness/
47. J. Alasdair Groves. Winston T. Smith, *Untangling Emotions*, (Wheaton: Crossway, 2019), 103.
48. Jennie Allen, *Untangle Your Emotions,* (Colorado Springs: Water Brook, 2024), 70.
49. Timothy Keller, *Counterfeit God,* (New York: Penguin RH, 2011), 17.
50. John Calvin and Henry Beveridge, *Institutes of the Christian Religion: Translated by Henry Beveridge* (Grand Rapids: Eerdmans, 1953), 1, II, 8
51. Bible Histories. "What was King Solomon Worth in Today's Dollars," YouTube, 03:43, posted February 21, 2024, https://youtu.be/CjkjzmZq7rA?si=JLsWpiEa7aepUmcG
52. Faith Driven Investor. "You Cannot Serve God and Mammon with Andy Crouch," YouTube, 0:10, March 10, 2022, https://youtu.be/8w4TQd_c85I?si=g8k4ScKdLXUXyGW3

53. Quote Fancy. "Hom Much Money Does It Take to Make One Man Happy?" *Quote Fancy.* https://quotefancy.com/quote/1388108/John-D-Rockefeller-How-much-money-does-it-take-to-make-a-man-happy-Just-one-more-dollar
54. Mission Self. "Why Self Storage is becoming a Booming Business in USA?" *Mission Self.* https://www.missionself-storage.com/why-self-storage-is-becoming-a-booming-business-in-usa
55. TEDx Talks, "The Battle for Your Time, Exposing the Costs of Social Media," YouTube, 03:00, posted March 6, 2023, https://youtu.be/4TMPXK9tw5U?si=diyn_OJDjUDEDylp
56. John Mark Comer, "Practicing the Way Podcast Episode 02: Be with Jesus," YouTube, 13:25, February 13, 2024, https://youtu.be/D99dQpuoEF4?si=ycOs97dq6tHyJCix
57. TEDx Talks, "Quit social media: Dr. Cal Newport," YouTube, 03:40, September 19, 2016, https://youtu.be/3E7hkPZ-HTk?si=Tv5Bcf0zkue9LEoR
58. Riendeau, Jerry. "FOBO: Gen Z's FOMO" *The Gospel Coalition*, January 8, 2023, https://www.thegospelcoalition.org/article/fobo-genz-fomo/
59. LifePlan. "The Porn Pandemic." *LifePlan.* https://www.lifeplan.org/the-porn-pandemic/
60. Smith, Morgan. "The No. 1 industry Gen Z wants to work in, according to new research—it's not tech" *CNBC*, November 14, 2023, https://www.cnbc.com/2023/11/14/the-no-1-industry-gen-z-wants-to-work-in-according-to-new-research.html
61. Michael John Cusick, *Surfing for God*, (Nashville: Thomas Nelson, 2012), 12-13.

62. Jerry Bridges, *The Fruitful Life*, (Colorado Springs: Navpress, 2006), 10.
63. Abide, "Christian Meditation Linked to Lower Stress & More," *Abide*. August 24, 2023, https://abide.com/blog/christian-meditation-linked-to-lower-stress-more/
64. Passion, "The Necessity of Awe- Ben Stuart // Passion 2023 Dallas/ Ft.Worth, TX" YouTube, 14:00, February 1, 2023, https://youtu.be/z0xuLTMrDqE?si=ApdOo1wheFAqjtDm
65. Tim Keller Sermons Message, "Unfallibale Joy" YouTube video, 15:08
66. Jerry Bridges, *The Fruitful Life*, 22.
67. Brother Lawrence. *The Practice of the Presence of God*, (Grand Rapids: Spire, 1967), 34.
68. Launay, Jacques. "Choir singing improves health, happiness – and is the perfect icebreaker," *Oxford University*. https://www.ox.ac.uk/research/choir-singing-improves-health-happiness-%E2%80%93-and-perfect-icebreaker
69. Brother Lawrence, *The Practice of the Presence of God*, 36.
70. Tim Keller, *Prayer: Experiencing Awe and Intimacy with God* (New York: Penguin, 2014), 228.
71. John Mark Comer, *The Ruthless Elimination of Hurry*, 155.
72. Ibid.
73. Gonzalez, Alden. ESPN, "Ippei Mizuhara, ex-interpreter for Shohei Ohtani, pleads guilty," *ESPN*. June 4, 2024, https://www.espn.com/mlb/story/_/id/40277006/ippei-mizuhara-ex-interpreter-shohei-ohtani-pleads-guilty
74. Health and Human Services. "The Epidemic of Loneliness and Isolation." *Health and Human Services*. https://www.hhs.gov/sites/default/files/surgeon-general-social-connection-advisory.pdf

75. Gilbert, Elizabeth. "Americans more than ever have no friends. Here are 5 steps to make more friends" *Big Think*, April 15, 2023, https://bigthink.com/neuropsych/americans-no-friends/
76. U.S. Department of Health and Human Services. *Our Epidemic of Loneliness and Isolation.* https://www.hhs.gov/sites/default/files/surgeon-general-social-connection-advisory.pdf.
77. Nicolaus, Paul. "Want To Feel Happier Today? Try Talking To A Stranger," July 26, 2019, *NPR*, https://www.npr.org/sections/health-shots/2019/07/26/744267015/want-to-feel-happier-today-try-talking-to-a-stranger?
78. Tony Reinke, *12 Ways Your Phone Is Changing You*, 60.
79. Goodreads. "Theodore Roosevelt Quotes," *Goodreads.* https://www.goodreads.com/quotes/6471614-comparison-is-the-thief-of-joy
80. Goodreads, "George W. Bush Quotes," *Goodreads.* https://www.goodreads.com/quotes/7746291-too-often-we-judge-other-groups-by-their-worst-examples
81. John Gordon, "Jon Gordon-No Energy Vampires Allowed," YouTube , March 13, 2014, 0:42, https://www.youtube.com/watch?v=PvYtpuZbvUw
82. John Gordon and Mike Smith, *You Win in The Locker Room First*, (Hoboken, John Wiley & Sons, Inc.: 2015), 35.
83. Scott Kennedy, "I Keep Receipts, You Better Get Me Right Now," YouTube, September 24, 2023, 0:44, https://www.youtube.com/watch?v=ho91tvyhmVg
84. Cru. "#ForgiveToForgive," Cru, https://www.cru.org/tt/en/communities/digitalministry/training/more/ready-to-use-content/forgiven-to-forgive.html

85. American Psychological Association, "Speaking of Psychology: How living with secrets can harm you, with Michael Slepian, PhD," *American Psychological Association*. https://www.apa.org/news/podcasts/speaking-of-psychology/secrets
86. Lib Quotes. "Ty Cobb Quotes," *Lib Quotes*, https://libquotes.com/ty-cobb/quote/lbe0o5u
87. CJ Mahaney, *Humility: True Greatness*, (New York: Multnomah, 2005), 29.
88. Gallup, "Church Attendance Has Declined in Most U.S. Religious," *Gallup*. March 25, 2024, https://news.gallup.com/poll/642548/church-attendance-declined-religious-groups.aspx
89. Hall, Jeffery. *Journal of Social and Personal Relationships,* https journals.sagepub.com/doi/pdf/10.1177/0265407518761225, 2019, Vol. 36(4)
90. Hall, Jeffery. *Journal of Social and Personal Relationships.*
91. Hellman, Rick. "How to make friends? Study reveals how many hours it takes," *Kansas University*. March 28, 2018, https://news.ku.edu/news/article/2018/03/06/study-reveals-number-hours-it-takes-make-friend
92. Harris Creek Baptist Church. "Life Groups," *Harris Creek Baptist Church*, https://www.harriscreek.org/lifegroups
93. Renovare. "Thou Shalt Celebrate: Excerpt from *The Spirit of Disciplines*" *Renovare*, https://renovare.org/articles/thou-shalt-celebrate
94. Matt Woodly, *Sunday's Best,* (Peabody, MA: Hendrickson Publishers, 2011), 234-235.
95. Running State. "At What Mile Do Most Runners Quit a Marathon," *Running State,* https://runningstate.com/at-what-mile-do-most-runners-quit-a-marathon/

96. Grace Quotes. "Joy-Suffering," *Grace Quotes*, https://gracequotes.org/topic/joy-suffering/
97. Boom, Corrie Ten. https://www.goodreads.com/quotes/248538-you-can-never-learn-that-christ-is-all-you-need
98. Tim Keller Sermons Message, "Infallible Joy" YouTube, 25:00, August 10, 2024, https://youtu.be/LEgJ0SZ3Rz0?si=5cabqZvAKfrsXhlX
99. Worldometer, https://www.worldometers.info/coronavirus/country/us/#google_vignette
100. Cru. "Today's Promise," *Cru*. https://www.cru.org/us/en/train-and-grow/spiritual-growth/devotionals/todays-promise/04/04.html
101. Lifeway Research. "Evangelism Explosion Study of American Christians Openness to Talking about Faith," *Lifeway Research*, https://research.lifeway.com/wp-content/uploads/2022/08/Evangelism-Explosion-Survey-of-American-Christians-Report-8_4_22.pdf
102. Earls, Aaron. "Christians Don't Share Faith with Unchurched Friends," *Lifeway Research*, September 9, 2021, https://research.lifeway.com/2021/09/09/christians-dont-share-faith-with-unchurched-friends
103. Lifeway Research. "Evangelism Explosion Study of Americans' Openness to Talking about Faith," *Lifeway Research*, https://research.lifeway.com/wp-content/uploads/2022/02/Evangelism-Explosion-Survey-of-Americans-Report.pdf
104. Martin B. Copenhaver, *Jesus is the Question: The 307 Questions Jesus asked and the 3 He Answered*, (Nashville: Abingdon Press, 2014), 119.

105. Quote Fancy. "Lottie Moon," *Quote Fancy*, https://quotefancy.com/quote/1650506/Lottie-Moon-Surely-there-can-be-no-greater-joy-than-that-of-saving-souls
106. Dave Earley and David Wheeler, *Evangelism Is: How to Share Jesus with Passion and Confidence* (Nashville: B&H Publishing, 2010), 13.

www.ingramcontent.com/pod-product-compliance
Lightning Source LLC
Chambersburg PA
CBHW070048100426
42734CB00040B/2610